# WITNESSES TO THE WORD

# WITNESSES TO THE WORD

## New Testament Studies
## Since Vatican II

DANIEL J. HARRINGTON, SJ

PAULIST PRESS
New York / Mahwah, NJ

The Scripture quotations contained herein are from the New Revised Standard Version: Catholic Edition Copyright © 1989 and 1993, by the Division of Christian Education of the National Council of the Churches of Christ in the United States of America. Used by permission. All rights reserved.

Cover background image of Dead Sea Scrolls courtesy of Gregor Buir / Shutterstock.com; cover photo of Qumran cave courtesy of Ella Hanochi / Shutterstock.com
Cover design by Sharyn Banks
Book design by Lynn Else

Copyright © 2012 by Daniel J. Harrington

Library of Congress Cataloging-in-Publication Data is available upon request

ISBN 978-0-8091-4820-2

Published by Paulist Press
997 Macarthur Boulevard
Mahwah, New Jersey 07430

www.paulistpress.com

Printed and bound in the
United States of America

To my brother, Edward J. Harrington,
with gratitude and affection

# Contents

Introduction ................................................................xiii

CHAPTER ONE: Interpreting the New Testament ................1

  1. The Bible as a classic text .........................................1

  2. The New Testament demands interpretation ..........2

  3. *Dei verbum*: An excellent framework for reading
     the Bible ..................................................................2

  4. Biblical interpretation and the hermeneutical
     problem .....................................................................5

  5. The major role of hermeneutics ...............................6

  6. Historical criticism: The world of the text and the
     world behind it ........................................................8

  7. New methods: The world before the text ..............10

  8. Theological exegesis ...............................................11

  9. Ways to do biblical theology ..................................12

 10. Biblical interpretation can and should enrich
     piety ........................................................................13

  Concluding Comment..................................................14

# CONTENTS

CHAPTER TWO: The Dead Sea Scrolls and Early Judaism....16

1. The importance of the discovery of the
   Dead Sea Scrolls .....................................................16

2. The Qumran library .................................................17

3. Writings contemporary with Jesus and the
   New Testament ......................................................18

4. Revivified study of the Greek Bible .........................19

5. Revivified study of the Apocrypha, or the
   Deuterocanonical books..........................................21

6. Revivified study of the Pseudepigrapha .................22

7. The Dead Sea Scrolls and other ancient Jewish
   writings.................................................................24

8. The Second Temple period .....................................25

9. Our changing perceptions about the history
   of Second Temple Judaism......................................26

10. Important parallels to Jesus and his movement ......27

Concluding Comment ..................................................29

CHAPTER THREE: Jesus, Prophet of God's Kingdom ...........30

1. Jesus as a historical figure .....................................31

2. Jesus in the historical context of first-century
   Judaism ................................................................33

3. The kingdom of God as his central theme .............34

4. Parables, maxims, debates, and symbolic actions....35

5. Miracles as signs of the kingdom .........................37

6. Jesus' teachings vis-à-vis the Jewish and Roman
   authorities.............................................................38

# Contents

7. Women in Jesus' public ministry ............................40

8. Pontius Pilate and the death of Jesus .....................41

9. Jesus was raised from the dead ...........................43

10. Books on Jesus by Joseph Ratzinger
    (Pope Benedict XVI) ...................................45

Concluding Comment ......................................46

CHAPTER FOUR: The Evangelists as Authors .....................47

1. From the death of Jesus to the first written
   Gospel—a forty-year gap ..............................47

2. Matthew, Mark, and Luke vis-à-vis the
   Gospel of John .......................................50

3. The Evangelists were authors ..........................52

4. The Two-Source Theory .................................53

5. The application of old and new methods ...............55

6. Mark: Jesus as the suffering Messiah .................56

7. Matthew: Jesus as a teacher ..........................57

8. Luke: Jesus as a prophet and an example .............58

9. John: Jesus as the revealer and revelation of God ...60

10. The so-called Apocryphal Gospels .....................61

Concluding Comment ......................................63

CHAPTER FIVE: New Perspectives on Paul and Judaism .....64

1. Paul in the context of first-century Judaism ...........65

2. Jews observed the law in the context of their
   covenant relationship with God .......................67

3. Paul's experience of the risen Christ trumped his past in Judaism...............68

4. Paul's conversion was from one form of Judaism (Pharisaic) to another (Christian)...........69

5. Paul did not set out to found a new religion separate from Judaism...........71

6. Could non-Jews be part of the people of God?.......72

7. The faith *of* Christ and the faith *in* Christ.............73

8. Paul's reasoning: From solution to plight.............75

9. "Works of the law" as identity markers of Judaism...........76

10. Paul and the salvation of "all Israel".............77

Concluding Comment.............79

CHAPTER SIX: Christians in the Roman Empire.............80

1. The Roman Empire as the larger context for Jesus and the early Church.............80

2. Attitudes toward the Roman Empire.............81

3. The Acts of the Apostles: The spread of Christianity in the Roman Empire.............83

4. Galatians and Romans: A Church of both Jews and Gentiles.............85

5. The Letter of James and Matthew's Gospel: The Jewish Christian voice in the Roman Empire.........87

6. Hebrews: Being a Jewish Christian in the Roman Empire.............88

## Contents

7. First Peter: Being a Gentile Christian in the Roman Empire .................................................. 89

8. First Corinthians: Problems facing Gentile Christians .......................................................... 91

9. The later Pauline letters: Coming to terms with the Roman Empire ...................................... 93

10. Philemon: Sociopolitical tensions with the Roman Empire ..................................................... 95

Concluding Comment .............................................. 96

Epilogue ..................................................................... 98

Glossary ..................................................................... 101

General Bibliography ............................................... 107

Index of Authors ..................................................... 115

Index of Scripture, Church Documents, and Ancient Texts ........................................................ 117

# Introduction

The Second Vatican Council (1962–65) coincided with my own formal beginnings in biblical studies. Taking the wise advice of a Jesuit dean who assured me that biblical studies was "the coming field" in Catholic circles, I began my study of Hebrew in the fall of 1962 when Vatican II was just beginning. I already had Greek and Latin down pretty well. Then, by writing summaries of articles and books, I first became associated with *New Testament Abstracts*, the journal published by the Jesuit theological faculty of Boston College, then in Weston, Massachusetts.

In the fall of 1965 (when Vatican II was ending), I began my doctoral program in the department of ancient Near Eastern languages and literature at Harvard University. My focus was on Second Temple Judaism, the period between Israel's return from exile in the sixth century BC to the destruction of the Jerusalem temple in AD 70. My expectation was that in order to understand the New Testament properly I had to first understand the Jewish world in which it was written. I already had the Greek and Latin classics down pretty well. In the fall of 1965, the final text of Vatican II's Dogmatic Constitution on Divine Revelation (*Dei verbum*) was issued. It was—and still is—the most comprehensive, most authoritative Catholic document on the interpretation of the Bible. It has shaped my life more than I ever imagined possible in 1965.

In the intervening years, I received master's degrees in philosophy and theology from Boston College and completed my doctoral degree at Harvard University. In postgraduate work at the Hebrew University and the École Biblique de Jérusalem, I studied under many of the best scholars of their generations. They treated the biblical texts both critically and respectfully, and gave me many good examples to follow. Through the years I have worked as a teacher and a scholar on ancient texts in Hebrew, Aramaic, Greek, and Latin. I have participated in the official edition of the Dead Sea Scrolls, with my teacher and friend John Strugnell. I have written over fifty books, some very technical and others intended for the general public. I have taught many courses and written hundreds of articles and book reviews on biblical languages, hermeneutics (that is, biblical interpretation), the late Old Testament, early Judaism, the Dead Sea Scrolls, the New Testament, and biblical theology. I have preached every Sunday on the assigned biblical texts. And I have loved every minute of it all.

One constant in all this activity has been *New Testament Abstracts*. I wrote my first abstract in the fall of 1962 on an article written in Latin, that had been published in an Italian journal, on the Apostolic Council, also known as the Jerusalem Council, as it is described in Acts 15. The article also suggested what might be expected from Vatican II in the light of Acts 15. Since then I have served as a regular contributor to the journal, now known as *NTA*, and have been its editor since 1972. I have written summaries of many thousands of articles and books.

In the late summer of 2011, I presented a major paper at the annual meeting of the Catholic Biblical Association entitled "New Testament Studies: Where Have We Been, and Where Might We Be Going?" Enrique Aguilar, the biblical editor at Paulist Press, suggested that I develop the paper into a short book coinciding with the fiftieth anniversary of Vatican II. His encouragement and persistence have turned that suggestion into a reality.

My task, as I see it, is to explain to a general audience what I regard as the most important developments in New Testament studies over the past fifty years. These are things, I think, that people should know. In one sense, this is a very personal book, and other scholars might do it quite differently. In another sense, it is an objective book because I am reporting on the work of many other scholars. I have divided the material into six chapters, focusing in each on what I consider one "big thing" in New Testament studies, and then relating that "big thing" to other developments in that general area of research. In each chapter I describe what I think represents some real scholarly progress since Vatican II, and about which ordinary people interested in religion and theology ought to know. In each chapter, I offer ten thesis statements that explain what these developments are and why they are important. Since to footnote every statement would defeat my purpose of reaching a general audience, I have added at the end of the book a general bibliography. In the main text I have placed the name of the relevant author or editor in bold type, along with a date if the person has more than one title attributed to him or her. It should be obvious from the context and from the title of the book in the general bibliography what the book is about. At the end of each chapter, I offer a concluding comment that mentions prospects and problems for future research. Finally, biblical quotations in the book are from the New Revised Standard Version.

In citing commentaries on the individual books of the New Testament, I have given special attention to the Sacra Pagina series (Liturgical Press), which I edited over many years (1988–2007). There are, of course, many other fine biblical commentaries. But this series was the first full-scale, English-language Catholic commentary on the whole New Testament. It took its name from the wish expressed in Vatican II's *Dei verbum* 24 that study of the "sacred page" be the soul of sacred theology.

While Vatican II is the starting point for this book, its scope is by no means narrowly Catholic. Since Vatican II, New Testament study has become increasingly ecumenical, with Catholic and Protestant scholars working together in generally harmonious ways. Moreover, in recent years there has arisen a substantial group of Jewish scholars dedicated to the study of the New Testament and its world, and they have made many impressive contributions to the field.

The title of this book, *Witnesses to the Word*, is based on the description of the Gospel writers in *Dei verbum* 19, which in turn alludes to Luke's description of his sources in the prologue to his Gospel (Luke 1:1–4). In the New Testament, the term *word* can refer both to the person of Jesus ("In the beginning was the Word," John 1:1) and to the good news about Jesus proclaimed by the early Christians and now preserved in the New Testament. Moreover, the modern scholars whose works are reported in this book are in their own ways witnesses to the word of Scripture in that they have devoted their lives to the serious study of the New Testament.

The subtitle of this book, *New Testament Studies Since Vatican II*, indicates that I am seeking to describe what can be learned from an academic or scholarly reading of the Bible, and to suggest some open questions that might be addressed in the future. My goal is to show that scholarly study of the New Testament is necessary and fruitful, and that a simplistic reading of Scripture does not do justice to its richness and will only impoverish both the text and the reader.

I regard this book as a roadmap to New Testament studies over the past fifty years. Throughout, I have tried to maintain a positive and constructive tone. There is nothing polemical or incendiary in it. I have long been convinced that there need not exist an "ugly ditch" between the academic's study of the Bible and the believer's devotional use of it. Rather, in keeping with the Catholic Church's recent official statements about the Bible and its interpretation, I believe that serious study of the Bible should both inform and enrich the life of the believer. That is my hope for this book.

I must acknowledge the support and friendship of my brother Ed, to whom this book is dedicated. I also thank the staffs of the oncology units at Mount Auburn Hospital in Cambridge, Massachusetts, and Beth Israel Deaconess Medical Center in Boston, Massachusetts, without whose care this book never would have been written.

# CHAPTER ONE

# Interpreting the New Testament

The Bible is really an anthology or collection of documents written by different authors living in different times and places. Yet over a fairly substantial period of time, first in the case of the Old Testament, and then with the New Testament, these disparate writings became part of the one book that we call the Bible. And that book has been and still is enormously influential in the lives of people all over the world. Thanks in large part to Vatican II's *Dei verbum*, Catholics and others have become more aware of the complexity and richness involved in interpreting the Scriptures, and have also come to recognize that there need not be a sharp division between the academic and spiritual readings of the Bible.

*Any* reading of the Bible must consider these ten key propositions about interpretation being put forth by today's scholars:

**1. The Bible has become a classic text.** A classic text is one that, over time, transcends the original circumstances of its composition. Homer's *Iliad* and *Odyssey* and Shakespeare's plays certainly qualify as classic texts. So does the Bible and, for our purposes, the New Testament.

The New Testament consists of four narratives about Jesus (the Gospels), a narrative about the spread of early Christianity (the Acts of the Apostles), thirteen letters attributed to Paul (the Pauline Epistles), a written sermon about Christ (Hebrews), seven more short letters attributed

1

to various apostles (the Catholic, or General, Epistles), and an apocalypse (Book of Revelation). What unites all these different writings is their focus on Jesus of Nazareth and the continuing significance of his life, death, and resurrection.

2. *The New Testament demands interpretation, just like any text.* Its twenty-seven books were all written in ancient Greek, but they have been translated into thousands of languages. Yet it is not enough merely to read the words on the pages of the New Testament. To understand these texts, we need to use our rational powers and engage in a critical analysis of them. The word *critical* here is not meant negatively, as if the interpreter's task is to point out errors in the Bible or to prove the Bible wrong. Rather, *critical* here means using our powers of understanding and reason to appreciate better the biblical text—where it came from, what it meant in its original historical circumstances, and what it might mean for people today. Using the official documents of the Catholic Church on the Bible and its interpretation, I believe that the Bible can and should be read both critically and religiously (**Marc Brettler**, **Peter Enns**, and **Daniel J. Harrington**).

3. *Vatican II's* **Dei verbum** *provides an excellent framework for reading the Bible both critically and religiously.* For Catholics at least, this document explains what the Bible is, how it is to be interpreted, and what role it should have in theology and church life. The title *Dei verbum* ("Word of God") comes from the first two words in its Latin text. In English, it is referred to as the Dogmatic Constitution on Divine Revelation. As a "dogmatic constitution" from an ecumenical council, it is a document of very high authority in the Catholic Church. At the Second Vatican Council (1962–65), the text was a topic of much controversy. But its final version passed by an overwhelming margin in the fall of 1965. Building on Pope Pius XII's 1943 encyclical

*Divino Afflante Spiritu* ("Inspired by the Holy Spirit"), it is the most complete statement about the Bible and its interpretation in the history of the Catholic Church (**Daniel J. Harrington, 2005**). Protestant and Jewish biblical scholars and theologians have also expressed admiration for much that is in it.

The text of *Dei verbum* (**Dean Béchard**, pp. 19–33) is divided into six chapters. The first chapter treats revelation in terms of God's personal self-revelation through the Old and New Testaments. It states that "by divine revelation God has chosen to manifest himself and to communicate the eternal decrees of his salvific will" (*DV* 6). The second chapter concerns the transmission of divine revelation. In dealing with the controversial theological issue of the relationship between Scripture and tradition, the document insists that they "are linked closely together and communicate with each other…flowing out of the same divine wellspring" (*DV* 9).

The third chapter deals with the divine inspiration and interpretation of Scripture. It stresses that Scripture was written both under the inspiration of the Holy Spirit and by human writers. The Bible is the word of God in human language, that is, the word of God in the words of men. On the one hand, interpreters must attend to the language, literary forms, and cultural assumptions in which the Bible was written. They must "search for what meaning the sacred writer in his own historical situation and in accordance with the conditions of his time and culture, intended to express and did in fact express with the help of the literary forms that were in use at the time" (*DV* 12). This statement affirms the validity of the historical approach to Scripture. On the other hand, the same paragraph insists that "Sacred Scripture must also be read and interpreted in the light of the same Spirit by whom it was written" (*DV* 12), thus leaving room for the spiritual or theological reading of the Bible as well. It explains the human and divine aspects of Scripture through the analogy of the incarnation. Just as Jesus could be both human and divine, so Scripture can be both human and divine.

Chapter 4 treats the Old Testament both as a source of great wisdom about God and human existence, and as a preparation for and a witness to Christ. The treatment of the Gospels in chapter 5 is especially important. On the one hand, the document affirms their basic historicity in faithfully handing on what Jesus did and taught. On the other hand, it recognizes the complexity of their composition: "The sacred writers selected certain of the many traditions that had been handed on either orally or already in written form; others they summarized or explicated with an eye to the situation of the churches" (*DV* 19). In other words, the Gospels passed through three stages: the time of Jesus, the time of oral and written traditions about Jesus, and the time of the Evangelists. The remaining New Testament writings are praised for their teachings about Christ, their proclamation of the saving power of his death and resurrection, their witness to the development of the early church, and their offer of hope regarding the fullness of God's kingdom.

The sixth and final chapter concerns the place of Scripture in the life of the church. It insists that all preaching should be nourished and ruled by Scripture, that easy access to Scripture should be available to all Christians, and that study of the "sacred page" (the Bible) should be the soul of theology.

Pope Benedict XVI has had a longstanding interest in the Bible and its interpretation. As a young theologian, Joseph Ratzinger wrote a substantial commentary on *Dei verbum*. As prefect of the Roman Congregation for the Doctrine of the Faith, he oversaw the development of, and wrote the preface to, the Pontifical Biblical Commission's 1993 document, "The Interpretation of the Bible in the Church," perhaps the best guide to the methods used in biblical studies today (**Béchard**, pp. 244–317; **Peter S. Williamson**). As pope, he convened a synod of bishops in 2008 under the title "The Word of God in the Life and Mission of the Church." The synod was intended as an examination of how *Dei verbum* had affected the life of the Catholic Church. In response, he issued in 2010 the apostolic exhortation entitled *Verbum Domini* ("Word of the Lord"), in which he insisted on the indispensable character of historical criticism, while affirming the necessity of theological or spiritual interpretation of the Bible (**Pope Benedict XVI**).

**4. Biblical interpretation involves confronting the hermeneutical problem.** The word *hermeneutics* means the "science of interpretation." The hermeneutical problem is, How do I get from there (an ancient text) to here (present-day life)? When applied to the Bible, the term can refer to the entire process of interpreting a biblical text (including its present-day meaning). Or, when used more narrowly, it can describe the attempt to move from the ancient text to an application of it for today.

The hermeneutical problem is present in many facets of life. We meet it in performing a play, or singing from a hymnbook, or reading a newspaper. What we have are words or signs on a page. They can be read (and interpreted) in many ways. For example, during the baseball season, the "Star-Spangled Banner" is performed at the beginning of every game. Over the course of the long season (162 games), it will be sung in many different ways. Which is the best way? Is there a best way? What does this or that performance try to express, not only about the song itself but also about life today? What are the criteria for judging a performance, for deciding whether it is good or bad?

The justices of the U.S. Supreme Court spend their days in hermeneutical reflection (**Jaroslav Pelikan**). Their job is to investigate the relationship between the U.S. Constitution and the law under discussion. They have to decide whether this or that law is in keeping with the Constitution, or whether it violates it. On the court itself, there will invariably be different interpretative approaches. The "strict constructionists" will focus on the original intent of the Founding Fathers and appeal heavily to the historical context of the Constitution in making their judgments. They tend to read their texts literally and historically. The "progressive" or "liberal" members of the court take the Constitution as it stands, and try to discern whether the law under consideration may be regarded as a legitimate development of what was written. They tend to look for the "spirit" of what they read in the Constitution, and to see how the law under consideration might be connected to, but developed from, the written text of the Constitution.

**5. Hermeneutics plays a major role in New Testament interpretation, even though it is properly the concern of philosophy.** For some biblical scholars, the hermeneutical task consists in determining as far as possible the meaning of the text in its original historical context. This is done by applying the tools of textual criticism and philology, as well as what can be known about the history of the period through archaeological excavations and contemporary writings. Then they might leave to themselves or to others the task of judging the ongoing significance of the text. For preachers and teachers, the hermeneutical task might be oriented more to the significance of the text for people today. They might read the text as it stands, and then use the text as a starting point for a discussion or a meditation or a homily.

Some philosophers and theologians distinguish the world behind the text, the world of the text, and the world in front of the text (**Sandra Schneiders**). Investigation of the world behind the text is the work of the historian, whose interest includes the culture, historical circumstances, and language in which the text was composed, as well as the events and concerns that led to its composition. The world of the text is the work of the literary critic, whose interests are the language and imagery of the text, the characters, the plot or structure, the literary form, and the message. The world in front of the text is the province of the believer, who prays on Scripture, as well as the religious educator and the preacher, whose concern is communicating the lasting significance of the text for people today.

While some New Testament scholars might focus on any one of these three aspects of the text, the ideal is to bring all three into play when interpreting a biblical text. Interest in the world of the text seems fundamental for everyone, unless one simply uses texts to reinforce one's already-existing ideas. The world behind the text calls for more specialized knowledge, and (however fascinating it may be) may also lead to fruitless speculation. The world in front of the text demands that the reader work seriously with the text in the hope that the encounter might bring about some kind of personal transformation.

The hermeneutical ideal is a fusion of horizons (**Hans-Georg Gadamer**). When we read a play script, a musical score, or a biblical text, we are dealing with an object that comes from the past, whether distant or fairly recent. It demands interpretation. It helps to be able to read the text intelligently (the world of the text), to know something about the historical context in which it was produced (the world behind the text), and to perform the text in a way that does justice to it (the world in front of the text). When the horizon of the text meets the horizon of the interpreter (be it actor, musician, or preacher) and when it issues in an appropriate performance (be it play, symphony, or homily/meditation), we have the fusion of horizons.

The modern study of the New Testament works within the framework of the hermeneutical problem as delineated by literary critics and philosophers. One of the most striking developments in New Testament study over the past fifty years has been the flourishing of various (mostly new) methods of interpreting biblical texts. No single one of these methods can tell the whole story of the text. Rather, they are ways of approaching the text in a rational and systematic (and respectful) manner in order to learn what the text meant in the past and may mean in the present and future.

**6. *Historical criticism concerns the world of the text and the world behind the text.*** What follows is a list (with definitions) of the various methods employed in the historical-critical study of the New Testament today (**Daniel J. Harrington, 1990**). It tries to show how and where they fit in the threefold schema of the worlds behind, of, and before the text. Some of these methods have been developed in other academic disciplines and adapted to New Testament study. Other methods are older and have long been in use in the biblical field. But even those have been reexamined and refurbished.

In dealing with the world behind the text, historical criticism remains indispensable—a word used frequently in recent Catholic documentation on the Bible. Historical criticism means placing a biblical text in its historical context (**John Barton**). This involves comparing a biblical text with other roughly contemporary ancient writings; investigating the historical circumstances of the period; discerning the presence of earlier source material within it; categorizing it in terms of the literary forms available to its author; calling upon the social sciences, such as cultural anthropology and psychology, to identify some of the sociological assumptions in the author's milieu; and hazarding a guess about what events lay behind the text.

Since the nineteenth century, archaeology has been an important tool in the historical criticism of the Bible. While archaeology can neither "prove" nor "disprove" the Bible on its own, it can give us an idea about how people in the biblical period conducted their everyday lives: what they ate and drank, what they wore, where they lived, and what they believed about themselves and God. These concerns and methods are not especially new. They have been developed and tested in various historical disciplines, and merit the title "indispensable" in the biblical field as well.

The study of the world of the text combines old and new methods. *Textual criticism* in biblical studies means gathering these ancient manuscript "witnesses" in Greek and other languages (Latin, Syriac, Coptic, and so on), and then trying to discern which may have been the original author's text, or at least trying to approximate the earliest form of the text. *Philology* (the study of languages) aims to establish the meaning and use of a word or phrase, and to determine what it means in a particular context. *Form criticism* deals with the distinctive literary form and genre of the text (parable, proverb, debate, and so on), and tries to determine how a correct recognition of the form can guide the interpretation.

The newer methods include *redaction criticism*, that is, why and how the biblical writer arranged his sources and what points he wanted to make in doing so. *Composition criticism* looks at the finished product that was the result of the editor's work. *Literary criticism* concerns the words and images of the text, its characters, structure, genre, and message. *Narrative criticism* considers the characters and their relationships, the plot, the narrator's point of view, the text's approach to time and space, and so forth. *Rhetorical criti-*

*cism* focuses on how the biblical authors used language and structure to gain the readers' attention and/or persuade them to feel something or do something. *Intratextuality* involves reading a text with reference to the final form of the document in which it stands—to its words and images, literary devices, form, structures, characters, and so on. *Intertextuality* investigates the links of a specific biblical text to other texts in the Bible or to texts outside the Bible.

**7. New methods focus on the world before the text.** The historical-critical method combines methods that pertain to the study of the world behind the text and the world of the text. But the process of interpretation does not end there. While indispensable, as I have said, it is not the whole story of biblical interpretation. In recent years, much greater attention has been given to the world before the text, the world contemporary to each interpretation—how the text has been and should be received, and how it may be actualized today.

The *history of interpretation* examines how a text has been understood by the great interpreters (Augustine, Jerome, Thomas Aquinas, Luther, Karl Barth) throughout the centuries. *Effective history* considers what effect, what impact, what influence a biblical text or book has had on church doctrines, history, art, literature, and so on. *Canonical criticism* is a theological program that seeks to establish a stance from which the Bible can be read as Sacred Scripture, to challenge the reader to look at the biblical text in its received, or canonical, form, and to discern its function for the community of faith. *Theological exegesis* focuses on the text's religious and theological thoughts and explores their implications for Christian theology and Christian life.

The term *actualization* refers to the process of bringing the significance of the biblical text into the present. In the 1970s, Latin American Christian "base communities" developed a three-step process of bringing Scripture into their present: (1) begin with an inspection of current social and political realities and their role in obstructing human flourishing; (2) move on to pertinent biblical texts and themes that might encourage the community to further thought and positive action; and (3) return to the community's current situation and then discern, in light of Scripture and prayer, how the community might act and move forward. This method was developed in the context of liberation theology in Latin America, and has been adapted by specific communities of women, African Americans, homosexuals, and poor persons in other settings.

*Feminist critique* of the Bible approaches the text with three major goals: to highlight as examples women who are portrayed positively (Mary Magdalene; Mary, the mother of Jesus; and others); to expose and challenge the patriarchy and hierarchy inherent in both Testaments; and to uncover the impulses toward human liberation in the Bible and use them in the process of rethinking the roles of women in the church and in society.

**8. Theological exegesis means taking with utmost seriousness the theological and religious concerns of the New Testament texts.** Perhaps a better term for *theological exegesis* is *theological reading*. This is what Pope Benedict XVI does in his books on Jesus of Nazareth. In some respects, this approach represents a reaction to the modern, massive commentaries that are stuffed with everything *except* theological and homiletic concerns. It takes its inspiration from the church's great commentary tradition represented by the church fathers, Thomas Aquinas, Luther, Calvin, and Karl Barth. While not ignoring totally the concerns of historical criticism, theological exegesis puts most of its energy into explication of the theological thoughts of the New Testament writers and their significance today.

**9. *There are many ways to do biblical theology.*** The obituary for biblical theology in general, and New Testament theology in particular, has been written many times. The most obvious problem is the sheer diversity of documents contained in the Bible. The Old Testament includes books written in Hebrew, Aramaic, and Greek, representing the wisdom of a thousand years. The New Testament contains the Gospels, Acts, the Epistles, and Revelation, written by many different human authors and in different places. And while these authors agreed about the pivotal significance of Jesus, they had different ways of expressing their beliefs and did not always agree with one another. Nevertheless, a glance at any issue of *New Testament Abstracts* will show that as an area in biblical studies New Testament theology is alive and well.

New Testament theology can take many forms. It can be a study of a word or a theme in one book (e.g., the word *poor* in Luke) or in several books (e.g., the phrase *kingdom of God* in the Synoptic Gospels). It can be a synthesis of the theological thoughts in John's Gospel or in Paul's Letter to the Romans. Or it can be the starting point in a theological argument about the divinity of Jesus or the common good.

Even more ambitious are the attempts at writing a theology of the New Testament as a whole. One approach (**Frank J. Matera, 2007**) moves from the individual writings to more general themes. Most of that work is devoted to describing the distinctive theological approaches in four major blocks of New Testament books: the Synoptic tradition, the Pauline tradition, the Johannine tradition, and other voices. Within those blocks, this work treats key theological perspectives in the individual writings: the kingdom of God (Mark), the righteousness of the kingdom (Matthew), the salvation that the kingdom brings (Luke), and so on. What sets Matera's approach apart is his effort then to go even further and to trace five master themes through the New Testament as a whole: humanity in need of salvation (anthropology), the bringer of salvation (Christology), the community of the sanctified (ecclesiology), the life of the sanctified (ethics), and the hope of the sanctified (eschatology).

A more traditional and yet more daring approach to New Testament theology is taken by the evangelical scholar **Thomas R. Schreiner**. He moves from the general to the particular. He argues that "magnifying God in Christ" can be taken as the master theme of the entire New Testament. He summarizes his work in this way: "NT theology is God-focused, Christ-centered, and Spirit-saturated, but the work of the Father, Son, and Holy Spirit must be understood along a salvation-historical timeline, that is, God's promises are already fulfilled but not yet consummated in Christ Jesus" (p. 23). His thematic approach is balanced by devoting separate sections to Matthew, John, and Paul as he develops various aspects of his main theme.

**10. Biblical interpretation can and should enrich Christian piety.** For many centuries, Christians have used the Bible in their prayer. Recent years have seen the adaptation of the monastic practice of *lectio divina* ("sacred reading") in ways in which it can be used either individually or in a group. It consists of four steps: reading the text slowly and reverently to understand it (*lectio*); reflecting on what it might be saying to me here and now (*meditatio*); asking God for what I need or want (*oratio*); and then either resting in the spiritual experience (*contemplatio*) or taking action (*actio*). A variation on this method is Ignatian contemplation, named after Ignatius Loyola, the founder of the Jesuits. This method involves entering into a Gospel scene by applying the senses and the imagination and asking: *What do I see? What do I hear? What can I touch? What do I smell?* and

*What do I taste?* The point is to become an active participant in the biblical narrative.

The most obvious forum for the actualization of Scripture is liturgy. In the Christian tradition going back to the church fathers, homiletics or preaching involves reading and interpreting a biblical text and bringing it to bear upon the situation of the congregation. Additionally, most church music is based on the Bible, especially the Book of Psalms and the Book of Revelation. The "Negro Spirituals" are uncannily perceptive in their interpretations of Scripture and their ability to present key biblical teachings in memorable and challenging ways. The challenge of *Dei verbum*—that Scripture be the soul of theology and at the heart of all preaching, teaching, and pastoral practice—remains a grand ideal to be actualized in many different ways.

***Concluding Comment***: For those seeking to read the Bible both critically and religiously, the recent Catholic documents on biblical interpretation (especially *Dei verbum*) provide a good model or framework, especially on the religious side. By accepting many of the key elements of the classic historical-critical method, *Dei verbum* encourages placing the biblical texts in their original historical contexts and grasping as best we can the original message of the biblical writers. There are many untapped riches in biblical texts, and the historical-critical method can help us to recover them. In particular, our appreciation of Old Testament texts may be greatly enriched by taking them more seriously on their own merits, rather than by forcing them into a "promise and fulfillment" christological schema (however valid that may be). By also insisting that the task of biblical interpretation does not end with determining the text's meaning in the distant past, *Dei verbum* challenges us to consider its significance for today and invites us to engage also in a religious or spiritual reading of it.

The questions involved with biblical theology are still alive and well: Should New Testament theology be simply the description of the theological thoughts of the biblical writers? Is it better to move from the particular to the general, or from the general to the particular? Is theological exegesis rigorous enough to merit the word *exegesis*? And is the canon of the New Testament more a source of diversity than of unity?

# CHAPTER TWO

# The Dead Sea Scrolls and Early Judaism

A foundational Christian belief is that "the Word became flesh and lived among us" (John 1:14). Christians believe that the Word became flesh in the person of Jesus of Nazareth, who lived as an observant Jew in Palestine, the land of Israel, between roughly 6 BC and AD 30. On a wider scale, he lived in the context of Second Temple, or early, Judaism, the period between the return from exile and the rebuilding of the Jerusalem temple in the sixth century BC, and the destruction of that temple by the Romans in AD 70 (**John J. Collins** and **Daniel C. Harlow**). The nature of that context has been greatly clarified by the discovery of the Dead Sea Scrolls and the subsequent reexamination of contemporary Jewish literature and history.

This "new" historical context of early Judaism, provided by the scrolls, has illumined both the world of the text and the world behind the text to a greater degree than ever could have been imagined in the past. The following ten theses sum up the scrolls' significance and are points to remember when reading the New Testament:

*1. The Dead Sea Scrolls may well be the most important archaeological discovery ever pertaining to the Bible and its world.* The term *Dead Sea Scrolls* actually refers to a series of discoveries that took place between 1947 and 1960. The most important site where ancient writings were found was Khirbet Qumran, not far from the Dead Sea. There, scrolls were discovered in eleven caves surrounding a central complex. The site was very early interpreted as the ruins of a Jewish religious settlement, and the scrolls were viewed as the remains of the library of a group known as the Essenes. The scrolls were dated between the second century BC and the first century AD. Thus, they have provided precious resources for understanding not only the life and times of a particular Jewish sect but also that of Judaism in Jesus' time (**James C. VanderKam; Geza Vermes**).

From the start, the Dominican Fathers at the École Biblique de Jerusalem were prominent in obtaining the scrolls, excavating the site, and organizing the publication project. Several Catholic scholars were part of the international and interconfessional team charged with identifying and editing the scrolls. As the team was expanded in the 1990s, many more Catholics became active in the project. The official publication of all the texts was spread over many years, and was brought to completion only in the 2000s, largely due to the learning, industry, and organizational skill of the Israeli scholar Emanuel Tov.

**2. The Qumran library has yielded the oldest texts of the Old Testament, as well as many other previously known and unknown Jewish writings.** Among the scrolls found at Qumran were the oldest manuscripts of the Hebrew Bible, some one thousand years older than anything previously known. All the books except Esther are represented, some in almost complete versions (the Book of Isaiah) and others only in tiny fragments. There are also commentaries on biblical texts (pesharim), Aramaic translations (Targumim), and imaginative rewritings (*Genesis Apocryphon*). Fragments of the original-language versions (in Aramaic or Hebrew) of such apocryphal works as *1 Enoch, Jubilees,* Tobit, and *Testament* *of Levi*, known previously only in various translations (Greek, Ethiopic, etc.), have been identified.

Most surprising among the Qumran scrolls were rule-books for life within a Jewish religious community, something like what developed into Christian monasteries. The *Rule of the Community* may have been the handbook for the group that lived at Qumran, while the *Damascus Document* seems to provide regulations for members in the larger society. Also included are a battle plan for apocalyptic warfare between the Sons of Light and the Sons of Darkness (*War Scroll*), a reworked version of certain provisions in the Bible (*Temple Scroll*), a large wisdom book (*4QInstruction*), a collection of poems (*Thanksgiving Hymns*), a treasure map written on copper plates (*Copper Scroll*), and what may have been a horoscope. These writings (apart from the *Damascus Document*) were totally unknown for two thousand years until their rediscovery at Qumran.

**3. *The Qumran scrolls are roughly contemporary with Jesus and the New Testament.*** The dating of the Qumran scrolls—from the second century BC to the first century AD—was established through archaeological excavations, study of the handwriting on the manuscripts (paleography), historical allusions in the texts (or lack thereof), and carbon-14 dating. While the site was initially identified as something like a monastery, there have been other interpretations: a military encampment for political insurgents, a commercial center on a trade route, a Jewish publishing center, a retreat facility, or a Roman villa. Some have even denied any connection between the buildings and the scrolls found in the caves. They argue that the scrolls represent the remains of a library connected with the Jerusalem temple and were brought to Qumran for safekeeping in view of the inevitable destruction of Jerusalem and its temple.

However, most scholars today hold to the very early

view that the Qumran scrolls are the remains of the library belonging to a Jewish group known as the Essenes, who inhabited the site and formed a religious community there. The movement most likely began in the struggle over the Jewish high priesthood in the mid-second century BC. The group seems to have been convinced that the priesthood and the temple were in the wrong hands (the Maccabees) and went out in protest to the Judean Desert until God might intervene on their behalf and restore control of the temple to them. They soon attracted a figure known as the Teacher of Righteousness, who became their spiritual leader. He might even have been the rightful claimant to the Jewish high priesthood. Thus, the community existed between 150 BC and AD 70, living as a Jewish sect with their own (solar) calendar and order of worship (the "sacrifice of praise").

**4. The Dead Sea Scrolls have revivified the study of the Greek Bible.** At Qumran and at other related sites, some fragments of the Greek Bible (also called the Septuagint) were found. Such texts are among the earliest extant manuscripts of the Septuagint and other ancient Greek versions, and research on them has greatly enriched our appreciation of the development of what were the first efforts at translation of the Hebrew Bible into another language and culture.

Perhaps even more important than the Greek manuscripts themselves were Hebrew biblical manuscripts that diverged slightly from the traditional Masoretic Text. Not only did they show that the Masoretic Text was not the only Hebrew text available in Jesus' time, but in some cases they also provided the Hebrew basis for renderings in the Septuagint that were once regarded as bad translations. The problem, scholars discovered, was not always with the Greek translator but rather with the different Hebrew texts on which the translation was based. Some scholars have tried to categorize the various Hebrew manuscripts into three major local categories (Palestinian, Babylonian, and Samaritan), while others are satisfied with even greater diversity.

Composed mainly at Alexandria in Egypt from the third century BC onward, the books of the Septuagint represent the first full-scale interpretation of the Hebrew Bible. Insofar as every translation is an interpretation, the Septuagint itself is an interpretation. The Dead Sea discoveries have led to a comprehensive study of the Greek Bible, with richly annotated translations in French, German, and English. The goal of many of these studies has been to analyze how Hebrew terms and concepts have been expressed in the Greek language, and the extent to which the thought of the Hebrew original has been changed (for good or ill), either deliberately or unconsciously in the light of Greek culture. These studies take the Septuagint on its own terms and approach the various non-Hebrew versions as precious witnesses to Second Temple Judaism outside the land of Israel.

The New Testament books were written in Greek and mostly (if not entirely) outside the land of Israel. This meant that the Septuagint was the Bible of the early Christians. Most of the biblical quotations in the New Testament come from the Septuagint. Many of the early translations of the Old Testament were made from the Septuagint. In Orthodox Christian circles, the Septuagint remains the official text of the Old Testament. Jerome broke the pattern by returning to the Hebrew text as the basis of his Latin translation. His example was followed by Martin Luther in his German version, with the result that Protestants follow the Hebrew text and restrict the books in their canon to what is in the Hebrew Bible. Among Catholic theologians, there used to be serious debates as to whether we should take the Septuagint (and not the Hebrew) as our Old Testament (following the example of the New Testament writers), and whether the Septuagint should be considered as divinely inspired. These debates have been revisited in recent years, and the topics are being taken even more seriously nowadays.

**5. The discovery of the Dead Sea Scrolls has revivified the study of other contemporary Jewish writings known as the Apocrypha, or the Deuterocanonical books.** While Jews and Protestants have limited their biblical canons to the Hebrew Scriptures, Catholics and Orthodox Christians have embraced a wider canon containing books found in the Greek Old Testament tradition. These additional books are sometimes called the Apocrypha or the Deuterocanonicals **(Daniel J. Harrington, 1999)**. In Catholic and Orthodox Bibles, they are interspersed among the undisputed Old Testament books, since they are considered canonical. In many Protestant Bibles, they are now presented in a separate section and identified as the Apocrypha. Whether or not they are considered canonical, they are now recognized by all as providing important background to the study of the New Testament.

Again the discovery of the Dead Sea Scrolls has provided a catalyst for more serious study of these books. Among the Qumran finds were large parts of the Book of Tobit in both Aramaic and Hebrew, and a few scraps of the Book of Sirach. A very large section of Sirach in Hebrew was discovered at Masada, the last Jewish outpost in the war against the Romans in AD 73.

While the so-called apocryphal books do not offer a complete or comprehensive view of Second Temple Judaism, they do preserve glimpses that enable us to get a better sense of the world out of which the New Testament emerged. The stories of Tobit and Judith are best understood as historical "novels." Tobit and his son Tobias constitute the ideal family living out the Jewish law in the Diaspora. Judith shows how God can use even the "hand of a woman" as his instrument in defeating the enemies of

Israel. The Book of Sirach (also known as Ecclesiasticus) is a huge wisdom instruction containing the teachings of a Jewish teacher active around 200 BC. His views on various topics are very useful for understanding the literary practices and the social and cultural assumptions of Jews even in Jesus' time. First and Second Maccabees provide abundant information about how Judea went from being part of the Seleucid Empire to being an independent nation state: First Maccabees tells how God used the Maccabee family—especially the brothers, Judas, Jonathan, and Simon—in bringing about Judean liberation and independence; Second Maccabees treats the background, events, and stories of individuals that led up to the Maccabean Revolt. The Book of Baruch shows how Jews used earlier biblical material in new settings. The Additions to the Book of Daniel and the Additions to the Book of Esther illustrate the tendency to expand writings and adapt them to new conditions. The Book of Wisdom, written in Alexandria around 50 BC, seeks to combine Greek philosophical concepts and Jewish biblical traditions. It is especially noteworthy for its emphasis on life after death, and on postmortem rewards and punishments: "The souls of the just are in the hand of God" (Wis 3:1).

**6. The discovery of the Dead Sea Scrolls has revivified the study of the Pseudepigrapha.** Among the Qumran scrolls were fragmentary manuscripts of writings known as the Old Testament Pseudepigrapha (**James H. Charlesworth**). The term means "written under a false name," a common literary practice in Jewish and Greco-Roman circles, intended to give greater authority to a writing by attaching its authorship to the names of Enoch or Moses, or of Plato or Aristotle. (Early Christianity would have its own pseudepigraphic writings, for example, some of the Pauline Epistles and works such as the *Gospel of Peter*, written about AD 190.)

The practice of pseudepigraphy probably reflects the emphasis on literary imitation in the schools of the period. The term does not fit all the Jewish works to which it is applied. Neither were all the writings that have been given that name found at Qumran. However, a few were, most prominently the work known as *1 Enoch*.

Prior to the Qumran discoveries, *1 Enoch* had been known through its lengthy Ethiopic version and through some fragments of a Greek version. But scholars had often supposed that it was originally composed in Aramaic or Hebrew. One of the most spectacular finds from Qumran Cave 4 were several fragmentary manuscripts of *1 Enoch* in Aramaic. Their presence proved the antiquity and popularity of the work at Qumran, and gave scholars the possibility of comparing the daughter versions (Greek and Ethiopic) with what seems to have been the original text.

*First Enoch* is a collection of materials associated with the figure of Enoch who "walked with God; then he was no more, because God took him" (Gen 5:24). This mysterious statement led some Jews to believe that Enoch had been taken into the heavenly realm and thus was privy to the mysteries of the universe and the future. The work known as *1 Enoch* is an anthology of materials connected with Enoch, and is usually divided into five "books." Fragments of materials from four of these books, plus excerpts from the related "Book of the Giants," are represented among the Qumran texts; however, the "Book of Parables" or "Similitudes of Enoch" (chapters 37–71) is missing. This section is famous for its references to the Son of Man and the Messiah. After a long debate, most scholars have concluded that this part was written in Aramaic in the first century AD, and that its absence from Qumran may be due simply to its relatively late date of composition in comparison with the other parts. So impressed were some scholars with *1 Enoch*'s presence at

Qumran that they have even posited the existence of a distinctively Enochic Judaism (apocalyptic and mystical) as opposed to Mosaic Judaism (Torah-oriented).

The Qumran discoveries have provided a stimulus for restudying these and many other works classified as pseudepigrapha in the light of the new picture of Second Temple Judaism that has emerged. A very full collection of these writings appears in the two-volume *Old Testament Pseudepigrapha*, edited by **James H. Charlesworth**. The writings include apocalypses (*2 and 3 Enoch, 4 Ezra, 2 Baruch, Apocalypse of Abraham*); testaments (*Testaments of the Twelve Patriarchs, Testament of Moses, Testament of Solomon*); rewritings and expansions of the Old Testament (*Jubilees, Joseph and Aseneth, Life of Adam and Eve*, ps.-Philo's *Biblical Antiquities*); wisdom and philosophical works (*Sentences of ps.-Phocylides, 4 Maccabees*); and psalms and prayers (*Prayer of Manasseh, Psalms of Solomon*).

**7. The discovery of the Dead Sea Scrolls has revived the study of other ancient Jewish writings.** In connection with the Qumran discoveries, the writings of Josephus—his autobiographical *Life of Josephus Flavius,* the *Jewish War*, and *Jewish Antiquities*—have been restudied and have proved to be precious resources for understanding the history of Second Temple Judaism, to the point that some scholars have called them "the Fifth Gospel" insofar as they present the historical background for Jesus and the early Christian movement in Palestine (**Per Bilde**). The writings of Philo of Alexandria illustrate how a Jew outside the land of Israel wrote in Greek and sought to bring together the Jewish biblical tradition and the basic concepts of Platonic philosophy (**Adam Kamesar**).

The rabbinic writings—the Mishnah and the Palestinian and Babylonian Talmuds (on how to behave in a proper Jewish fashion), the Midrashim (Jewish Bible commentaries), and the Targumim (Aramaic translations and expansions of biblical texts)—are full of information about Jewish life in antiquity (**Hermann L. Strack** and **Günter Stemberger**). However, they do present a dating problem for use in New Testament study. They were compiled, it seems, between AD 200 and the seventh century. However, they do contain traditions that are much older and often provide striking parallels to New Testament texts. One growing area in Qumran studies is comparing the legal and exegetical material in the Dead Sea Scrolls and in the classic rabbinic works to see what is similar and what is different (and why).

**8. Once a neglected area in archaeological research in Israel, the Second Temple period has become a very lively topic**. Again Qumran provided the impetus. Soon after the discovery of the scrolls at Qumran, the Dominican Roland de Vaux undertook a systematic excavation of the central site. He interpreted the evidence as supporting the initial hypothesis that it was the remains of a Jewish religious community that lived a kind of monastic existence there, and that the scrolls found in the surrounding caves were the remains of the community library, perhaps stashed there for safekeeping in the face of a Roman assault in AD 73 or 74. The same evidence, however, was interpreted in other ways, and so the controversy about the nature of the central site and the relationship of the scrolls to it continues even today.

However one judges de Vaux's work (and I agree with it for the most part), the excavations at Qumran certainly stimulated to a large extent the field of Second Temple archaeology. The discovery of inscriptions in Hebrew, Aramaic, and Greek has provided precious evidence for understanding the linguistic situation in Palestine in Jesus' time. Excavations all over the land of Israel have revealed much about where and how the common people lived, and even what they wore, ate, and drank (**Jodi Magness**). The ancient "Galilee boat" recovered from the Sea of Galilee during a drought gives a sense of what Jesus' first followers used in their work as fishermen. While mainly from a period well after Jesus and the New Testament, the many synagogues excavated in Palestine have greatly enriched our appreciation of the social and religious life of Jews outside of Jerusalem and its temple. The origin of the synagogue remains a debated issue, but the references to synagogues in the New Testament provide some of the earliest evidence for their existence. The many excavations conducted in Jerusalem have given a sharper picture of what the city and its temple were like in Jesus' time. The reconstruction of how crucifixion was administered on the basis of the bones of a man who had been crucified showed how Jesus might have met his death on the cross. The excavation of tombs (mainly burial caves) and in them the discovery of ossuaries ("bone boxes") have greatly illuminated the Gospel accounts of the burial of Jesus and the empty tomb on Easter morning. Thus, there are many cases in which archaeology illuminates the New Testament, and the New Testament illuminates archaeology.

**9. Our perceptions about the history of Second Temple Judaism have changed through study and restudy of the literary and archaeological evidence.** Rather than viewing Jews as existing in a kind of hermetically sealed temple state, it has become increasingly clear that, to a large extent, Jews in Palestine were influenced long before Jesus' time by the Greek/Hellenistic world in the form of language, economics, administration, military strategy, and culture (**Martin Hengel, 1974**). Even those like the Maccabees who supposedly opposed Greek culture adopted many features of it for themselves. Moreover, Jewish communities were spread all over the Mediterranean world (the Diaspora), and there was a great deal of communication between them and the motherland.

Second Temple Judaism was a time of ongoing political conflict. When Jews were under foreign domination (from the Persians, the Seleucids, the Ptolemies, the Romans), religion was a rallying point. In times of relative Jewish independence (under the Maccabees and the Herods), it was often a point of contention. What united Jews was the Torah (the Jewish Law, or the Pentateuch), the Jerusalem temple, and the land of Israel. But even these matters were controversial in some circles. Indeed, there were different ways of being a Jew: Pharisee, Sadducee, Essene, Samaritan, Zealot, and Christian.

**10. The Dead Sea Scrolls have provided important parallels to Jesus and his movement.** Despite the claims of some irresponsible scholars, the Qumran texts never mention or refer to Jesus. Most of Jesus' public activity occurred in Galilee, far from Qumran and the Dead Sea. Jesus was never identified as an Essene. In fact, mention of the Essenes is curiously absent from the New Testament. If there was a link between the Jesus and the Qumran people, it may have been through John the Baptist. What the Dead Sea Scrolls do provide are parallels to Jesus and the New Testament. Keeping in mind that in geometry parallel lines never meet, nonetheless, we can expect to find from the scrolls some of what was "in the air" in the Judaism of Jesus' time (**Daniel J. Harrington, 2007**).

The Qumran people shared the hopes of other Jews and of Jesus for the full manifestation of God's kingdom. The presence of multiple copies of Daniel and *1 Enoch* bear witness to their interest in apocalyptic thinking. While none of the "sectarian" works at Qumran are apocalypses, many of these texts contain apocalyptic language and content. For example, the *War Scroll* is a verbal blueprint for a cosmic battle between the Sons of Light and the Sons of Darkness, which will issue in the kingdom of God. The Master's instruction in the *Rule of the Community* envisions a divine visitation in which the righteous Sons of Light will be vindicated and enjoy eternal life while the wicked will be destroyed forever. Some texts indicate that the people of Qumran considered themselves as living in "the last of days." Several of the wisdom texts speak frequently about "the mystery that is to come," presumably somehow connected with the full coming of God's kingdom. And, as in the New Testament (see Rev 4–5), they also believed it possible in the present to enter the heavenly council in a mystic way through prayer and liturgy.

The *Rule of the Community* describes the ritual washings (baptisms) that members underwent regularly; an appendix to it envisions the community meals as the "messianic banquets" at which the Messiah of Aaron and the Messiah of David preside. Despite their expectations of an imminent end of times, the Essenes had a hierarchical community structure, with the Guardian or Overseer and the Teacher at the head, and a kind of executive committee consisting of three priests and twelve laymen. Like Jesus and the early Christians, they had some ambivalence about the Jerusalem temple. While respecting the institution, they were convinced that it was in the wrong hands and wished for a new, better temple.

A major figure in the history of the Qumran group seems to have been a person referred to in several texts as the Teacher of Righteousness. Some of the *Thanksgiving Hymns (Hodayot)*, written in the first-person singular, have been interpreted as his autobiographical reminiscences. He may have been the legitimate high priest ousted by the Maccabees, who then turned to the Essene community around 150 BC and became its major spiritual leader. Like Jesus, he was regarded as a recipient of divine revelations about the mysteries of God and his kingdom, and he provided wise teachings and spiritual leadership by which he was remembered with reverence. He suffered from opponents within the Jewish community, and yet his movement continued. The major difference was that the followers of Jesus proclaimed that he had been raised from the dead, and that that he now reigns as "Lord Jesus Christ."

***Concluding Comment***: Despite all the great accomplishments in the study of the Dead Sea Scrolls and the other documents of early Judaism, its practitioners acknowledge that we still see "in a mirror, dimly" (1 Cor 13:12). A major emphasis in this area of study has been to demonstrate the great diversity within early Judaism. However, the old question remains about what, if anything, held early Judaism together. Was it simply the trio of "land, law, and temple"? Or do we need something even more unifying, something like a "common" or "normative" Judaism? Do we have only a set of marginal fragments that have been preserved accidentally? And how do we relate the traditions preserved in the rabbinic writings to early Judaism and to the New Testament?

These are old questions. But they take on new urgency in light of the many positive achievements in the study of the Qumran scrolls in particular and early Judaism in general.

# CHAPTER THREE

# Jesus, Prophet of God's Kingdom

The last part of the twentieth century saw an explosion of books and articles about Jesus. Perhaps it had something to do with the approach of the year 2000. Perhaps it was the need to find in Jesus a justification for the increasingly common self-identification of people as "spiritual, but not religious." Perhaps it was the need to get straight the relationship between Jesus and the Jewish people, especially in light of the European Holocaust. Whereas around the time of Vatican II, New Testament scholars were concerned with showing what was different about Jesus from his Jewish contemporaries, in more recent times the focus has been on locating Jesus within Judaism.

This trend has been called the "Third Quest of the Historical Jesus," and has brought to the fore Jesus' identity as the prophet of the kingdom of God. The "First Quest" refers to attempts, mainly in the nineteenth century, to isolate the *real* Jesus, the *historical* Jesus, from the Gospel accounts of him and the church's theological traditions. The so-called "Second Quest" in the mid-1900s was especially concerned with capturing Jesus' self-consciousness on the basis of certain sayings in the Gospels. While the first two quests were carried out almost exclusively by German-speaking Protestant scholars, the Third Quest—locating Jesus within Judaism—has been international and interconfessional.

When reading the New Testament with an eye toward Jesus as a first-century Jew—a real person within a real time and place—there are ten key points to keep in mind; and within those points, scholars take some different approaches:

**1. Despite serious obstacles, it is possible to speak with confidence about Jesus as a historical figure.** The difficulty involved in this undertaking starts with the fact that Jesus lived 2000 years ago in what we call Palestine/Israel. He left no writings in his own name. Those who did write about him at length (the Evangelists) did so some forty to sixty years after his death. These writers were convinced that Jesus of Nazareth was much more than a simple Jewish teacher. Indeed, they believed that he had been raised from the dead and now lived in heaven with the one whom he had called "Father."

If it is difficult to write the biography of any person, how much more difficult it must have been to write about the one whom the Evangelists and other believers regarded as the Messiah, the Son of God, the Lord. Moreover, these same writers were not as interested in the plain facts of Jesus' life as they were in his ongoing significance for them and their communities.

The quest for the historical Jesus usually refers to the project of separating the earthly Jesus from the Christ of faith (**Albert Schweitzer**). The historical Jesus is the historian's Jesus, that is, the actual man who can be "reconstructed" through use of the tools of modern historical research. The quest started among liberal German Protestants in the late eighteenth century. Their goal was to describe the "real" Jesus as a figure in human history, and to peel away the theological veneer that the early church and the Evangelists had allegedly placed over him. Thus, they dismissed the miracles as well as the virgin birth and the resurrection as "unhistorical." The resulting Jesus was a high-minded but unsuccessful and somewhat deluded Jewish political revolutionary. Two positive contributions from the nineteenth-century quest were the recognition that Mark is the earliest Gospel and that the kingdom of God was the focus of Jesus' preaching and activity.

In the twentieth century, the quest first focused on the parables as a privileged way of hearing the "voice" of Jesus, especially his way of teaching about the kingdom of God. Then it turned to developing criteria for distinguishing material that came from Jesus from material produced by the early church and the Evangelists. In more recent times, this focus has been on Jesus' relationship to Judaism, and his identity as a prophet, a sage, and a poet.

Even using the historian's criteria (without the negative philosophical presuppositions), it is nevertheless possible to develop a credible portrait of Jesus' life and teaching (**John P. Meier; E. P. Sanders, 1985; N. T. Wright, 1997**). Having been raised in Nazareth, Jesus accepted baptism from John the Baptist and may have been a member of John's movement. He then went out on his own, attracted followers near the Sea of Galilee, preached about the coming kingdom of God, and healed sick and possessed persons as a sign of the presence of that kingdom. Around Passover in AD 30, he and his followers made a long journey from northern Galilee to Jerusalem, where he briefly continued his ministry. There he encountered fierce opposition from various Jewish groups and the Roman authorities, and was crucified as a dangerous rebel and a religious troublemaker. After his death, his close followers affirmed that they had experienced him as alive again.

At the center of Jesus' teaching was the kingdom of God in both its future and its present dimensions. In this context he proclaimed the possibility of the forgiveness of sins and reconciliation with God. His own relationship with

God was so intimate that he called him "Father" and invited his followers to do the same. He challenged his followers to love their enemies, and taught them how to conduct themselves in anticipation of the coming kingdom. He demonstrated a special concern for marginal persons—the poor, the lame, sinners and tax collectors, prostitutes, and so on—and took a somewhat free attitude toward the traditions connected with the Jewish law and the Jerusalem temple.

However valuable this historical outline of Jesus' life and teaching may be, it is not the whole story about him **(Daniel J. Harrington, 2007)**. The Jesus whom Christians from earliest times named "Lord Jesus Christ"—and proclaimed Messiah, Son of Man, and Son of God—transcends the narrow vision of the secular historians. The Jesus of the Gospels is the one whom the early Christians remembered and interpreted in the light of their belief in his resurrection from the dead. They did not distinguish sharply between the Jesus of history and the Christ of faith.

**2. Jesus must be understood in the historical context of first-century Judaism.** The Word became flesh (John 1:14) in the land of Israel/Palestine/the Holy Land. The western border of that region is the Mediterranean Sea, and the eastern border is the Jordan River. The land is usually divided into three sections. To the north is Galilee, where Jesus spent most of his life. Then, as now, it was prominent for farming and fishing. The area around the Sea of Galilee was the site of much of Jesus' public ministry. To the south is Samaria, a district generally avoided by Jews, but prominent in several Gospel episodes (John 4:1–42; Luke 10:25–37). Further south is Judea with its traditional capital, Jerusalem, and its religious center, the temple. While John presents several visits to Jerusalem by Jesus, the Synoptic Gospels (Mark, Matthew, and Luke) describe only one visit, which issues in Jesus' death.

The land of Israel in Jesus' time was part of the Roman Empire. The Herod family exercised control over most of the land, which was a "client state" of the Romans. At the time of Jesus' birth (6 BC), Herod the Great was still in control. When Jesus died (AD 30), Herod Antipas ruled over Galilee, and the Roman prefect or governor, Pontius Pilate, ruled directly over Judea.

According to Matthew and Luke, Jesus was born in Bethlehem, the city of David, not far from Jerusalem. Luke 2 describes the child Jesus being "presented" in the Jerusalem temple, and Jesus and his family making a pilgrimage to Jerusalem from Galilee at Passover. Jesus was clearly raised in Nazareth, a small village in the middle of Galilee. He is said to have had "brothers and sisters" (Mark 6:3), probably cousins or stepbrothers and stepsisters. He seems to have learned the trade of carpentry or small construction.

Jesus apparently had a traditional Jewish upbringing and came into adulthood as an observant Jew. At least in the early part of his public ministry, Jesus frequented the local synagogues. While he had a somewhat free attitude toward the traditions surrounding Jewish law, he seems to have been generally observant of the law itself. He did not belong to any of the major Jewish religious movements of the time (Pharisees, Sadducees, Essenes, or others), although he at least shared an agenda with the Pharisees. He did accept "baptism" from John the Baptist and seems to have been part of that movement for a while. And according to the Gospel of John (chapter 1), the Baptist's disciples provided Jesus with some of his earliest followers.

**3. *The kingdom of God was the central theme of Jesus' teaching and activity.*** When introducing Jesus as a public figure, Mark summarizes his teaching in this way: "The time is fulfilled, and the kingdom of God has come near; repent, and believe in the good news" (1:15). The kingship of God is prominent in many Old Testament psalms (e.g., "The LORD is king!" in 97:1), and the proposal that Israel should have a human king like other nations posed a crisis of conscience between proponents and opponents. After the Babylonian exile in 586 BC, when Israel no longer had a human king, there arose the hope for a glorious future in which the wise and righteous might be vindicated. The different scenarios for such a kingdom appear in the Book of Daniel, some Dead Sea Scrolls, and other works known as apocalypses (*1 Enoch, 4 Ezra, 2 Baruch*). In some cases the messiah ("the anointed one") is a major figure.

In Jesus' life and teaching, the kingdom of God is both future and present. The future dimension is captured neatly in what is called the Lord's Prayer: "Your kingdom come. Your will be done on earth as it is in heaven" (Matt 6:10). It is also prominent in many of his parables that begin, "The kingdom of God/heaven is like...." The present dimension is expressed in various sayings such as, "Then the kingdom of God has come to you" (Luke 11:20), and "The kingdom of God is among you" (Luke 17:21). In John's Gospel, the focus of Jesus' teaching is his role as both the revealer and the revelation of God, which suggests that Jesus is the embodiment of God's kingdom. In his life and teaching, we have the anticipation and inauguration of the fullness of God's kingdom. In theology, the kingdom with its *already* and *not-yet* aspects is the horizon of Christian life.

**4. Jesus taught about God's kingdom through parables, maxims, debates, and symbolic actions.** As an effective teacher, Jesus promoted his vision of the kingdom of God in various ways (**Ben Witherington**). One of the most obvious ways was the parable. A parable is a story about nature or everyday life that has some surprising or unusual element that makes the hearer suspect it is really about something more than it seems on the surface. It makes the hearer wonder what that might be. Many scholars argue that in the parables we hear the voice of Jesus most clearly and purely.

In Mark 4, Matthew 13, and Matthew 24 and 25, several parables begin with the phrase "The kingdom of God is as if…" or "The kingdom of God is like…." Their topics—how seeds grow, the tiny mustard seed, the weeds and the wheat, the yeast in the flour, the buried treasure, the precious pearl, and fishermen sorting their catch—fit perfectly well in the context of Galilee in the first century. As a wise teacher, Jesus used familiar material from nature and everyday life to help his Galilean contemporaries grasp what he was saying about the kingdom of God. For example, the mustard seed (Mark 4:30–32) is very small, but it grows into a very large bush. Here Jesus seems to be contrasting the small beginnings of God's kingdom in his own person and ministry (the already) with what will be its grand conclusion in the fullness of God's kingdom (the not-yet). He affirms that while something significant is happening in the present, the best is yet to come. In the meantime, the proper attitude is constant fidelity and vigilance. The beautiful parables of the Good Samaritan (Luke 10:30–37) and the Prodigal Son (Luke 15:11–32) illustrate Jesus' teachings about love of enemies and God's willingness to forgive sinners, respectively.

To many in his time, Jesus looked and acted like a Jewish wisdom teacher. In proclaiming the present and future of the kingdom of God, he used many of the devices and addressed many of the topics found in the Old Testament wisdom books of Proverbs, Sirach, and Ecclesiastes. For example, in the Sermon on the Mount in Matthew 5–7, we have a collection of Jesus' sayings arranged by the Evangelist (or a source) into what looks like a Jewish wisdom instruction. It begins with the Beatitudes, and declares some unlikely persons to be happy or blessed. It then uses the metaphors of salt and light to describe those who accept Jesus' teachings. It uses contrasts or antitheses to show how Jesus goes to the root of various Old Testament teachings. It provides rules for the proper attitudes in almsgiving, prayer, and fasting. Then, from Matthew 6:19 through all of chapter 7, it treats various topics (treasures, the sound eye, the futility of worry, the hypocrisy of judging others, and so on), and presents these teachings in the forms of prohibitions, maxims or proverbs like the Golden Rule ("do to others as you would have them do to you"), and warnings to practice what Jesus preaches. All of these wisdom teachings appear in the context of the narrative about Jesus and his proclamation of God's kingdom.

The Gospels often portray Jesus in debate or controversy with other Jewish teachers. His major debating partners are the scribes and Pharisees. While he sometimes agrees with them, mostly he displays his superior wit and authority—and wins out. For example, in the debate about paying taxes to the Roman emperor in Mark 12:13–17, Jesus escapes the trap set by his hostile opponents, and declares that those who use Caesar's coins are already part of his system, but that the "system" of God is even more important and deserves more attention. As the prophet of God's kingdom, Jesus also uses the device of symbolic actions. Good examples include the "triumphal" procession into Jerusalem on Palm Sunday and his "cleansing" of the Jerusalem temple (see Mark 11:1–11, 15–19). Both accounts are full of Old Testament overtones, and surely got Jesus in trouble with both the Jewish and Roman political authorities.

**5. *The miracles of Jesus are best understood as signs of the presence of God's kingdom.*** The Gospels are full of reports about Jesus as a miracle worker. According to one estimate, they contain (not counting repeated passages) seventeen healings, six exorcisms, and eight nature miracles

(**John P. Meier**). Almost a third of Mark's Gospel is devoted to Jesus' miracles, and the first half of John's Gospel features seven "signs" or miracle accounts. And of course, the resurrection of Jesus is the greatest miracle of all.

In common speech today, a miracle is an event that is an exception to the laws of nature, or at least one for which there is no natural explanation. Whether one attributes it to God depends largely on one's philosophy or worldview. In the Bible, however, miracles are understood more broadly as signs of God's power at work. Therefore, in the Gospels, the miracles are not so much proofs of Jesus' divinity as they are signs of the presence of God's kingdom at work in the person of Jesus. The key to understanding the miracles of Jesus comes from his words preserved in Luke 11:20: "But if it is by the finger of God that I cast out demons, then the kingdom of God has come to you." Even the opponents of Jesus admitted that he performed miracles. Their complaint concerned the power by which he performed them (see Mark 3:22–30). They suspected that he was a kind of magician in league with the devil. In response Jesus accused them of blaspheming against the Holy Spirit.

**6. *Jesus' teachings had political and economic implications that got him into trouble with the Jewish and Roman authorities.*** Jesus was a prophet of God's kingdom and a wisdom teacher, not a politician or an economist. In his time, however, religion and politics were not neatly separated, and there was only one real kingdom (the Roman Empire) and one real king (the emperor). So when Jesus proclaimed the future coming of God as king over all, he was saying provocative and dangerous things.

By the time of Jesus, the people of Israel had lived under many different political systems. In the age of the biblical judges (1200–1000 BC), there was a loose confederacy of the twelve tribes bound together by a covenant. In the age of the monarchy (1000–586 BC), first there was one king over all (David and Solomon), and then a divided monarchy in which the northern kingdom of Israel fell to the Assyrians in late eighth century BC and the southern kingdom of Judah that fell to the Babylonians in early sixth century BC. After the return from exile, the Judeans lived under a series of foreign empires: Babylonian, Persian, Greek, and Roman. From the mid-second century to the late first century BC, the Maccabees brought a version of independent Jewish rule, although their alliances with the Romans led to Judea becoming one more segment in the Roman Empire. Some scholars (**Richard A. Horsley**) see Jews in this period existing in "a spiral of violence" in which popular resistance led to further oppression, and more resistance ultimately leading to full-scale insurgency and the destruction of Jerusalem and its temple in AD 70.

While there is no evidence that Jesus was in sympathy with violent Jewish revolutionary movements, his teaching about God's coming could and did sound revolutionary. In the Gospels, the closest Jesus comes to commenting on the Roman Empire comes in the "render to Caesar" passages (Mark 12:13–17; Matt 22:15–22; Luke 20:20–26). The question put to Jesus is, "Is it lawful to pay taxes to the emperor, or not?" If he says yes, he gets in trouble with the religious-oriented insurgents for supporting the foreign oppressors. If he says no, he is liable to be reported to the Roman officials and arrested. He escapes the dilemma by challenging his questioners to be as careful about paying their obligations to God as they are in paying taxes to Caesar (**Christopher Bryan**).

On economic matters, Jesus stood in the great biblical traditions of social justice and concern for the poor (**Leslie Hoppe**). In his own teachings about rich and poor, there are three basic strands. According to the first strand, poverty can be a positive personal good because the poor may be better able to recognize their dependence on God and to focus on the service of God rather than competing for earthly goods. The second strand suggests that riches and possessions can be obstacles to serving and attaining God's kingdom. And the third strand emphasizes the need for those who are rich in this world's goods to share their material possessions with the poor of the world. These were hardly the social values of the Roman occupiers.

7. **Women played important roles in Jesus' public ministry.** The Jewish world in which the Word became flesh was both hierarchical and patriarchal. Roles and tasks were clearly divided between men and women, with men having the more public and authoritative positions. In the family, the husband was the head, and the women, children, and slaves were subordinate to him.

For the most part, Jesus and his first followers were people of their times, that is, hierarchical and patriarchal. However, there are hints that their movement was more open than most Jewish groups to the participation of women (**Elisabeth Schüssler Fiorenza**). In Luke's infancy narratives, women—Elizabeth, Mary, and Anna—are major figures. The way in which Jesus' mother Mary is portrayed in Luke 1–2 makes her the first and best example of Jesus' own definition of his ideal disciple: "those who hear the word of God and obey it" (Luke 11:28).

According to Luke 8:2–3, the band of Jesus' followers included several prominent women—Mary Magdalene, Joanna, Susanna—as well as "many others." We can presume that these women traveled with Jesus and the male disciples and witnessed his healing and teaching activity, something that would have looked very strange in their historical context. According to Luke 10:38–42, Jesus declares Mary's desire to listen to Jesus' teaching as "the better part" in comparison with her sister Martha's busyness with more conventional domestic tasks. In the passion narratives, the women followers remain faithful to Jesus, in contrast with his male disciples. The women see Jesus die, they see him buried, and they find his tomb empty on Easter Sunday. According to both Matthew and John, the first recipient of an appearance of the risen Jesus was Mary Magdalene. Her commission to tell the male disciples about Jesus' resurrection has merited for her the title of "apostle to the apostles."

In the course of Jesus' public ministry, women were often the objects of his healing powers: Peter's mother-in-law, the daughter of Jairus, the woman with the flow of blood, the daughter of the Syrophoenician woman, and the crippled woman of Luke 13:10–17. Jesus' absolute prohibition of divorce (Mark 10:2–12) gave some protection to women who otherwise could be dismissed simply at the husband's whim (Deut 24:1–4). There is no evidence that Jesus had a wife, and his own words suggest that he undertook voluntary celibacy out of his dedication to the kingdom of God (Matt 19:10–12).

**8. Pontius Pilate, with the cooperation of some Jewish officials, was responsible for the death of Jesus.** The passion narratives in the four Gospels agree that around Passover time, probably in AD 30, Jesus was arrested, underwent two hearings or trials, was sentenced to death, and was crucified. Mark's account seems to be the earliest, and was in turn expanded by Matthew and Luke independently. John's narrative represents a separate tradition; while highly literary and theological, it contains many reliable historical points **(Raymond E. Brown, 1994, 1999)**. The tendency in these accounts is to heighten the guilt of the Jewish leaders (scribes, elders, and chief priests) and to play down the role of the Roman prefect/governor, Pontius Pilate. John goes so far as to lump all of Jesus' opponents under the title of "the Jews."

However, a careful reading of these sources indicates that Pilate had the principal legal responsibility in the execution of Jesus. The manner of Jesus' death (crucifixion), the legal system in force (Pilate having the power of execution), the official charge against Jesus ("king of the Jews"), and those who were crucified along with him (thieves, bandits, rebels, revolutionaries), all point to the conclusion that the ultimate moral and legal responsibility for Jesus' death lay with the Roman prefect, Pontius Pilate. It appears that Pilate viewed Jesus as just another in a long line of Jewish religious insurgents, and followed the Roman strategy of administering swift and brutal "justice." Why he did not arrest Jesus' followers and also have them killed remains a mystery.

Although Pilate bears primary responsibility for Jesus' execution, it appears that he had cooperation from some of the Jewish leaders in Jerusalem. The Evangelists describe them as the chief priests, elders, and scribes. Note that there is little or no mention of the Pharisees in the passion narratives.

Jerusalem was a pilgrimage center in Jesus' time. Three times in the year—at Passover, Weeks, and Tabernacles—pious Jews were expected to come to the holy city and its temple. That meant large crowds would descend on the city and perhaps present problems of crowd control. Passover, of course, commemorated the Jews' escape from slavery in Egypt in Moses' time, and had obvious political overtones for a people under Roman domination. When Jesus and his disciples came to Jerusalem for Passover in AD 30, staged a "triumphal" procession worthy of the Messiah, and demonstrated against the commercial corruption associated with the temple sacrifices, these events spelled danger for both the Roman and the Jewish authorities. It was in their mutual best interest to keep the peace. And that peace appeared to be threatened by Jesus.

The Gospels recount trials (or hearings) about Jesus before the Jewish leaders. According to Mark, there were two charges: that Jesus threatened to destroy the temple, and that he claimed to be the Messiah and Son of God. There is very likely some basis for these charges. Not only had Jesus "cleansed" the temple, but also according to Mark 13:1–2, he prophesied its imminent destruction. Likewise, it appears that Jesus' authoritative style of teaching and his many miracles had led some to speculate whether he might indeed be the Messiah and Son of God. Ironically, Jesus accepts these titles (plus Son of Man) only at the least likely moment in his trial before the Sanhedrin (Mark 14:61–62).

The question of responsibility for Jesus' death has a long and sorry history. In some Christian circles, it led to the charge against the Jews of *deicide*, that is, since Jews killed Jesus and Jesus was divine, therefore, the Jews killed God. Such reasoning led some Christians through the centuries to imagine that they had the right and permission to kill Jews. Modern biblical scholarship has established convincingly enough that Pilate bore the ultimate legal responsibility for Jesus' death. The question among scholars has been the extent of Jewish cooperation. Without attempting to decide that issue, the Second Vatican Council did state that "neither all Jews indiscriminately at that time, nor Jews today, can be charged with the crimes committed during [Jesus'] passion" (*Nostra aetate* 4).

**9. Jesus was raised from the dead: this was the boldest and most important claim that early Christians made.** Resurrection means the restoration of the whole person to life after death (**N. T. Wright, 2003**). It is not same as resuscitation, since it is assumed that resuscitated persons will die again. It is also not the same as immortality of the soul, since that would involve the separation of the soul from the body.

The early parts of the Old Testament bear witness to a belief in life after death. It was believed that the dead went to the abode of the dead called Sheol and lived a kind of shadowy existence. The prophets Isaiah and Ezekiel used resurrection as a metaphor to express their hope that the defeated and exiled people of God might rise to new life. The Book of Daniel looked forward to the time when "many of those who sleep in the dust of the earth shall awake, some to everlasting life, and some to shame and everlasting contempt" (12:2). Similar ideas about resurrection can be found in 2 Maccabees 7 and the Book of Wisdom.

Those Jews in Jesus' time who believed in resurrection thought that it would be a collective event, preceding the Last Judgment and involving eternal life for the righteous and punishment or even annihilation for the wicked. The great proponents of resurrection were the Pharisees, and in this matter Jesus agreed with them. In Mark 12:18–27, he argued against the Sadducees, affirmed that reference to resurrection can be found in the Book of Exodus, and said that resurrected life is not the same as earthly life.

The three elements in the New Testament's approach to the resurrection of Jesus are the empty tomb, the appearances, and the transformation of Jesus' disciples. All four Gospels agree that on Easter Sunday morning, women who saw Jesus die and saw him buried found his tomb empty. Of itself, the empty tomb does not prove the resurrection of Jesus. But it is a necessary precondition of it. More convincing are the many appearances of the risen Jesus to those who knew him when he was alive and who knew that he had died. These appearance stories occur at the end of each of the four Gospels, as well as in a list that is part of a very early confession of faith in 1 Corinthians 15:3–8. And perhaps the strongest proof of all is the remarkable transformation that came over the disciples. Disciples who had earlier fled his side or even denied knowing Jesus now became public witnesses to his resurrection and its significance.

Those who do not believe in the possibility of resurrection have to explain away each of these elements. For those who do believe, these elements work together to serve as the basis of their faith.

**10. The books on Jesus by Joseph Ratzinger (Pope Benedict XVI) represent an affirmation of Dei verbum and a challenge to New Testament study today.** In the first volume of his Jesus of Nazareth books, **Joseph Ratzinger** covered events in the Gospels from Jesus' baptism to his transfiguration. In the second volume, he focused on the events of Holy Week. Never before had a reigning pope written such a book, and he even claimed to welcome criticisms of his work.

These books are not a biography of Jesus, an exegetical exposition of the Gospels, or a systematic treatise on Christology. Rather, they are a form of biblical theology, or theological exegesis, a series of learned reflections on various episodes and aspects of the four Gospels. They combine historical exegesis, patristic theological insights, more recent theological concerns, liturgical practice, and contemporary experience. They use the Old Testament as a means toward understanding New Testament passages. The pope interprets Scripture using Scripture, and looks to the sacramental and liturgical implications of the biblical texts. In short, he illustrates how one interpreter can apply the principles of *Dei verbum*.

From the start, the pope makes clear his principles of biblical interpretation. They are not shared by all New Testament scholars, but they are stated clearly and concisely. He contends that the portrait of Jesus in the Gospels is trustworthy, and that it (and not some modern historian's reconstruction) is the proper object of study and devotion.

45

In short, the historical Jesus *is* the Jesus of the Gospels. Jesus is the key to interpreting all the Scriptures, and so the Bible as a whole can and should be read from a christological/canonical perspective. The historical-critical method is foundational and indispensable but not completely adequate for understanding Jesus and the Scriptures.

***Concluding Comment***: What have we learned from the Third Quest of the Historical Jesus? On rereading Schweitzer's work on the First Quest, one might conclude that there are not many things said in the recent incarnation of the quest that were not somehow already present in its earlier incarnations. However, there has been in much of the Third Quest a new and much sounder emphasis on first-century Palestinian Judaism as the proper historical context for understanding Jesus' life and teaching. The problem now is, So what?

Certainly any serious historical study is worth doing for its own sake. However, Pope Benedict XVI has raised some issues that biblical scholars today need to take seriously. He is rightly skeptical about what can be achieved by going behind the texts of the Gospels to reconstruct the "real Jesus." Rather, his starting point is the Jesus of the Gospels; and while he attends to Jesus' historical context, his major interest is the theological significance of this Jesus, not some speculative reconstruction made by this or that modern historian.

# CHAPTER FOUR

# The Evangelists as Authors

The traditional picture of an Evangelist sitting at his writing desk composing one of the Gospels while taking dictation from the Holy Spirit is no longer an adequate expression of how the Gospels came to be. Likewise, an earlier scholarly view of an Evangelist simply piecing together little traditions like pearls on a string is equally inadequate. As *Dei verbum* 19 insists, the Gospels have to be read at three levels: Jesus, the early church, and the Evangelists. The inspiration of the Holy Spirit comes both at the communal level (the process of oral and written tradition) and at the individual level (the work of each of the Evangelists). While the material in the Gospels has passed through a complex process of transmission, those who finally formulated it and set it in a narrative context can legitimately be called authors. Each presents a distinctive interpretation of Jesus, and so each deserves that title.

Any consideration of the authorship of the Gospels must include an awareness of the human elements involved. The following ten thesis statements provide a focus for understanding the major aspects of Gospel authorship:

*1. Between the death of Jesus and the first written Gospel (Mark), there was a gap of forty years.* Most scholars agree that Jesus was put to death around AD 30 and that Mark's Gospel was composed around AD 70. What happened in between? The early Christians seem not to have had much interest in writing books. They were more concerned with living out their newfound faith and bearing witness to others about its transforming power. They met regularly and practiced the rituals of baptism and Eucharist. They emphasized the need for ethical behavior appropriate to their religious convictions. Their religion seemed peculiar to their neighbors, especially since they did not practice material sacrifices of animals, food and drink, and so on (**Gerd Theissen**).

What was foundational to the early Christians was their beliefs about Jesus of Nazareth (**Raymond E. Brown, 1994**). They were convinced that he had died for the sins of others (including themselves) and thus had atoned for them. They were convinced that God had raised him from the dead. They were convinced that he now reigned in glory with his heavenly Father and that he would come again. This is what they meant by the word *gospel* (which already had a background in Second Isaiah and in Roman imperial propaganda). It was the "good news" (*euangelion*) about Jesus and the saving significance of his death and resurrection that most interested and animated them. By the time of the earliest written New Testament document—1 Thessalonians in AD 50—it had become customary to refer to Jesus as "the Lord Jesus Christ." The text of that Pauline letter shows how quickly belief in Jesus and his saving significance developed, to the point that one scholar (**Martin Hengel, 1983**) described it as not a development but an explosion.

The good news about Jesus found expression in short summaries of faith and in early Christian hymns. When writing to the Corinthians around AD 55, Paul reminds them that what he taught them is what had been handed on to him: "that Christ died for our sins in accordance with the scriptures, and that he was buried, and that he was raised on the third day in accordance with the scriptures, and that he appeared to Cephas, then to the twelve" (1 Cor 15:3–5). This confession not only highlights the events of Jesus' death and resurrection; it also provides a theological interpretation of them: Jesus' death was an expiation for our sins, and both his death and his resurrection were in accord with the divine plan revealed in the Old Testament. Other such short summaries of early faith can be found in Paul's words to the Galatians: "All of you are one in Christ Jesus" (Gal 3:28); and to the Romans: "Christ Jesus, whom God put forward as a sacrifice of atonement by his blood" (Rom 3:25). Such summaries become even more frequent in the Pastoral Epistles (Titus, and 1 and 2 Timothy).

In writing to the Philippians in the mid-50s of the first century AD, Paul in 2:6–11 quotes an early Christian hymn about Christ Jesus as the Servant of God (see Isaiah 53 for the background). The hymn first describes the incarnation as Christ emptying himself of divinity and taking human form, even to the point of death on the cross. Then it describes his exaltation (beginning with the resurrection) and the proclamation by all creation that "Jesus Christ is Lord." Likewise in Colossians 1:15–20, there is an early Christian hymn that celebrates Christ as the wisdom of God (see Proverbs 8, Sirach 24, and the Book of Wisdom for the background). The hymn describes Christ as Wisdom personified, present both before and at creation ("the firstborn of all creation"), and then portrays him as first in the order of redemption ("the firstborn from the dead") through whose death God has reconciled all things to himself. Jesus is both "head" of the church and the cosmic redeemer.

As time went on, there seems to have been more interest in preserving and gathering the teachings of Jesus himself. It appears that teachings from and about Jesus circulated in small units in early Christian circles, first in oral form and then in written form. The discourse forms include parables, proverbs or maxims, warnings, "I" sayings, and rules. Among the narrative forms are healings, exorcisms, and nature miracles. A mediating form is the controversy or conflict story in which Jesus' opponents pose a question or set a trap, and he displays his superior wit in the form of a wise saying.

As these small packets circulated, they began to grow into larger blocks of material. For example, the five accounts of Jesus as a miracle worker and a wise teacher in Mark 2:1—3:6 probably were put together and sent to Mark as a large unit. Some scholars think that even the Sermon on the Mount in Matthew 5–7 might have come to the Evangelist as a unit. Likewise, the passion narratives in all four Gospels are surely based on traditional material. The seven "signs" of Jesus in John 2–12, as well as material in the Farewell Discourses in John 13–17, probably reflect material developed in the Johannine school or circle.

Interest in the origin or birth of Jesus probably came even later. Mark has no infancy narrative. It starts abruptly with Jesus as an adult. Matthew's infancy narrative focuses on Jesus' roots in ancient Israel's history and takes Joseph as the main character. Luke's infancy narrative focuses on Mary, and contrasts John the Baptist and Jesus. The point is that even as an infant John the Baptist was great, but Jesus was greater still. And in the prologue to his Gospel, John traces the origin of Jesus to the time before creation ("in the beginning was the Word"), thus identifying him in terms of Wisdom personified.

*2. The Gospels of Matthew, Mark, and Luke present a common vision (synopsis) of Jesus, while John reflects a different tradition.* The first three Gospels are often called the Synoptic Gospels because they offer a common vision of Jesus in their outline of his public ministry, of the titles applied to him, and of the wording in many passages. Their similarities (and differences) can best be seen with the help of a synopsis, a book that places the texts of the three (or four) Gospels in parallel vertical columns.

In describing the public ministry of Jesus, the Synoptic Gospels follow a common outline: after accepting baptism from John and exercising a ministry of teaching and healing in Galilee, Jesus and his disciples make a journey from northern Galilee to Jerusalem, where he teaches for a brief period, is arrested, and is put to death. If the Synoptics were the only gospels, we would imagine that Jesus' ministry lasted for one year and that this was the only time he went to Jerusalem as an adult. The three Synoptic Gospels depict Jesus as a teacher and healer, and use the common stock of honorific titles about him: Christ/Messiah, Son of Man, Son of David, Son of God, and Lord. The ease with which they use these titles when referring to Jesus is yet another example of the theological "explosion" that occurred very early in Christian circles. And in many places, the verbal similarities are so close (e.g., Matt 3:7–10 and Luke 3:7–9) as to suggest the use of a common source or copying from one Gospel by another.

John is different. In the Fourth Gospel, Jesus makes several trips to Jerusalem, and his ministry is spread over three Passovers and thus three years. In this, the Johannine tradition is very likely correct historically. The Johannine Jesus teaches by means of long discourses, not the short units that make up the Synoptic Gospels. There is also a different set of characters in John's Gospel: Nicodemus, the Samaritan woman, the man born blind, Lazarus, and the Beloved Disciple. The focus of Jesus' teaching is not so much the kingdom of God as it is his own identity as the revealer and revelation of God. While there are some overlaps between the Synoptic and Johannine traditions, it is not clear that John knew any of the Synoptic Gospels directly.

**3. *The Evangelists were authors.*** As we have seen, the word *gospel* (*euangelion*) originally referred in Christian circles to the good news about Jesus and his saving death and resurrection. When Mark introduced his work with "The beginning of the good news (*euangelion*) of Jesus Christ, the Son of God," he began (whether consciously or not) a tradition that changed the meaning of the word *gospel* into a literary genre, that is, a narrative about Jesus' life and death. Now when we hear the word *gospel*, we most often think of Matthew, Mark, Luke, and John. And what they have in common is their literary character as narratives about Jesus of Nazareth.

Technically the four Gospels are anonymous compositions. In their main texts, no one names himself as the author (as Paul does in his letters or John does in Revelation). The labels "According to Mark" and so on seem to have been introduced in the second century, and may or may not rest on solid historical traditions. However, it is customary in modern New Testament study to refer to each of the four Gospels by the traditional names of Matthew, Mark, Luke, and John.

Calling the Evangelists "authors" demands some qualifications. They were not like modern fiction writers who create their narratives out of their own imaginations; rather, they stood in a rich theological tradition and already had access to oral and written traditions about Jesus (see Luke 1:1–4). Neither were they like modern editors who compile existing traditions into an anthology; rather, as we will see, they used their traditions with great care and literary finesse. Nor were they like modern biographers, who are primarily concerned with the facts about their subjects. Ancient biographies were more concerned with the moral and exemplary significance of their subjects. And to some extent the four Gospels fit that model. However, the

Evangelists wanted to say much more about Jesus' significance ("Lord Jesus Christ") than their contemporaries said about their subjects, even if they were emperors.

The Gospels are sometimes described as "portraits" of Jesus. A portrait is not the same as a photograph. There is more room for interpretation in a portrait. These portraits are based on the reminiscences of Jesus' first followers, and so they present us with "Jesus remembered" (**James G. D. Dunn**). These memories have passed through a process of transmission in which they may have been adapted to the needs and concerns of later Christians. The achievement of the Evangelists was to incorporate the traditional material into their distinctive portraits and to bring out specific dimensions of Jesus' person that they regarded as especially appropriate for their readers. To that extent they can be called authors.

As *Dei verbum* 19 insisted, the Gospels have to be read at three levels: Jesus, the early church, and the Evangelists. This following conciliar statement captures exactly the complexity of the process by which the Gospels were composed: "In composing the four Gospels, the sacred writers selected certain of the many traditions that had been handed on either orally or already in written form; others they summarized or explicated with an eye to the situation of the churches. Moreover, they retained the form and style of proclamation but always in such a fashion that they related to us an honest and true account of Jesus."

**4. The Two-Source Theory is the most economical and widely accepted hypothesis about the relationships among the Synoptic Gospels, that is, Matthew and Luke both, although independently, used Mark and Q, and then individually they each used some special traditions.** The Synoptic Problem arises from the fact that many teachings and episodes appear in all three Synoptic Gospels (triple traditions), some occur in two Gospels (double traditions), and some in only one (special material). In most cases of the triple and double traditions, the wording is so close as to suggest some relationship of direct dependence. Augustine thought that Matthew was the first Gospel, that Mark was a poor imitation, and that Luke used them both. A late-eighteenth-century German scholar named J. J. Griesbach contended that Matthew was first, Luke second, and Mark third. However, as the nineteenth century progressed, scholars came to believe that Mark was the oldest complete Gospel, and that it served as a source for both Matthew and Luke. That explained most of the triple traditions.

To explain the double traditions, scholars hypothesized that a collection of Jesus' sayings in Greek which they named "Q" (from the German word for "source," *Quelle*) was used independently by both Matthew and Luke. According to this theory, those two Evangelists also used material unique to their Gospels designated as "M" and "L," respectively. For example, most of the Sermon on the Mount in Matthew, and the parables of the Good Samaritan and the Prodigal Son in Luke, appear only in one Gospel.

In my thesis statement on the Two-Source Theory, I used the word *hypothesis* advisedly, in order to indicate that not everyone agrees with what is now practically a consensus solution. The most obvious problem is that no one has ever seen Q. Rather, it is a scholarly reconstruction based on the material in the double tradition. Moreover, throughout the centuries Matthew, not Mark, was assumed to be the earliest Gospel. And there are some loose ends and "minor agreements" that do not fit the general framework of the Two-Source Theory. Indeed, it is likely that a more complex solution would explain even more of the evidence. However, despite the learned objections of some, the Two-Source

Theory remains the most economical and widely accepted solution to the Synoptic Problem.

**5. The application of old and new methods has enriched the interpretation of the Gospels.** Having recognized the complexity of the process by which the Gospels were composed, we need methods of interpretation that will be appropriate to their character and that will help in entering the world of the text. In analyzing a specific text, basic *literary criticism* is a good first step. (More sophisticated methods of analysis are *semiotics* and *structuralism*.)

Literary criticism begins with the words and images in the text: What might they mean in this context? Do they appear elsewhere? Do they have a significant history? A second concern might be the characters: Who are they? How do they relate to one another? Who is the most important? A third concern would be the structure or plot of the text: How does the action move? What is the climax? What is the result? A fourth concern would be the literary form: Is it a discourse or a narrative? Is it a parable or a controversy story? Is it a maxim or an admonition? The final issue is the message of the text: What is the point? What might this text have been saying to people in the first century? What might this text be saying to people today? Trying to see where a text fits and functions in the whole plan of a Gospel is a form of *narrative criticism*.

To get to the world behind the text, *source criticism* is important: Is it possible to ascertain that a Gospel text depends on an earlier source? In the triple and double traditions, it is easy enough to know when Matthew or Luke was using Mark or Q. The Evangelist's adaptation of the source is called *redaction* or *editorial criticism*. In other cases, the unusual vocabulary or thoughts, or an awkward transition, might indicate the use of a source. The original intent of *form criticism* was not only to categorize the literary forms that appear in the Gospels but also to reconstruct the history of the early church on the basis of how the individual forms might have functioned. And more recently, the Jesus-questers have developed a set of criteria for discerning with some certainty what in the Gospels goes back to the historical Jesus: dissimilarity with regard to Judaism and early Christianity, multiple attestation in several sources, Palestinian coloring in language and customs, embarrassment to early Christians (e.g., Peter's denial of Jesus), and so on.

With regard to the world before the text, a focus on the religious significance of the text (*theological exegesis*) is an obvious starting point. Viewing the text in connection with other biblical texts is a form of *canonical criticism*, which can also be called *intertextuality*. Examining how the text has influenced people throughout the ages is called *effective history*. And of course, how the text might be used in prayer, preaching, and artwork remains the goal of much biblical study today, and is sometimes called *actualization*.

In the next four thesis statements, I will characterize each Gospel's distinctive portrait of Jesus, and describe its structure and its distinctive approaches to Christology, discipleship, and eschatology. It is primarily in this sense that the Evangelists can be called authors.

**6. *Mark emphasizes Jesus as the suffering Messiah.*** Written around AD 70 at Rome (or perhaps in southern Syria), Mark's Gospel (**John R. Donahue** and **Daniel J. Harrington**) falls into three major parts: Jesus' activity as teacher and healer in Galilee (1:1—8:21): Jesus and his disciples' journey from Galilee to Jerusalem (8:22—10:52): and Jesus' ministry and death in Jerusalem (11:1—16:8). The pivotal moment in the outline comes in Mark 8:29 when Jesus elicits from Peter the confession "You are the Messiah." In some Jewish circles there was the hope that God would send a religious, political, and military leader like David, and he would restore Israel to its place of international prominence. What Peter and the other disciples have to learn is that Jesus is not that kind of messiah. Rather, he is a Suffering Messiah, and they will not understand Jesus' messiahship until they confront the mystery of the cross. That is the "messianic secret."

In Mark, the disciples start off well. They respond immediately to the call of Jesus, and fulfill the Markan ideal of discipleship as being with Jesus and sharing in his mission. However, instead of growing in faith and knowledge, they become increasingly obtuse. Even though Jesus instructs them in Christology and discipleship on their journey, they fail to understand his three predictions about his passion, and flee at the moment when Jesus most needs a friend in the passion narrative. By contrast, the women disciples who are introduced only in 15:40–41 remain faithful to Jesus. They watch him die, they see where he is buried, and they go to his tomb only to find it empty. With regard to eschatology, Mark keeps a balance between the already (1:15) and the not-yet (13:1–31); he urges constant watchfulness (13:32–37) as the proper attitude toward the coming of the glorious Son of Man.

*7. **Matthew emphasizes Jesus as a teacher.*** Written around AD 85–90 in Antioch of Syria, Matthew's Gospel **(Daniel J. Harrington, 1991)** follows the three-part outline in Mark (Galilee–journey–Jerusalem) but adds the infancy narrative at the beginning and the appearances of the risen Jesus at the end. But the most impressive additions are the five speeches of Jesus (occurring throughout chapters 5 to 7, 10, 13, 18, and 24 to 25), which he intersperses between narrative sections. The result is to heighten Jesus' prominence as a teacher. In the Sermon on the Mount (Matt 5–7), Jesus instructs his hearers on the virtues, attitudes, and behaviors that are appropriate to those in search of the kingdom of

God. In the Missionary Discourse (10), he invites the disciples to share in his mission, and explains what they might expect, how they might react along the way, and how they should respond to rejection. In the Parables Discourse (13), he uses many different analogies to explain what he means by the kingdom of heaven. In his Community Discourse (18), he offers counsel about problems that might arise within the community of followers, and stresses the importance of the willingness to forgive one another. And in the Eschatological Discourse (24–25), Matthew takes over much material from Mark 13, but then also provides several more parables about constant watchfulness and presents a judgment scene in which Jesus the glorious Son of Man presides and judges according to acts of kindness toward "the least."

Matthew upgrades the image of the disciples somewhat from Mark. They are the chosen students of Jesus the teacher, and they understand much of what he says. However, at several moments they are characterized correctly as having "little faith." That is better than having no faith at all, but it is far from perfect faith. On the one hand, Peter in his failure to continue walking on the water is criticized by Jesus as the model of "little faith" (Matt 14:31). On the other hand, he is praised by Jesus as the recipient of a divine revelation about his true identity (16:17–19). The several parables that Matthew adds at the end of chapter 24 and throughout chapter 25 add to the Mark's message of vigilance in the face of the apparent delay in the full coming of God's kingdom.

*8. Luke emphasizes Jesus as a prophet and an example.* Written around AD 85–90 perhaps in Greece, Luke's Gospel (**Luke Timothy Johnson, 1991**) also follows Mark's three-part outline (Galilee–journey–Jerusalem), and adds an infancy narrative at the beginning and appearances of the risen Jesus at the end. His major innovation is the expansion of the journey narrative into more than ten chapters (Luke 9:51—19:27) compared to the two and a half chapters in Mark. There he includes much material that is unique to his Gospel: the Good Samaritan, Mary and Martha, the Prodigal Son, and Zacchaeus.

Luke's Jesus is first and foremost a prophet. A prophet is someone who speaks for God. The prophecies of Zechariah and Simeon about the infant Jesus suggest that as an adult he will be the fulfillment of the Old Testament prophecies. In Jesus' inaugural discourse in Luke 4:16–30, he reads from the Book of Isaiah and declares that "today this scripture has been fulfilled in your hearing." Jesus goes on to appeal to the examples of Elijah and Elisha as prophets who brought their healing powers to Gentiles. When he restores to life the son of the widow of Nain, the crowd rejoices that "a great prophet has risen among us" (7:16). In the episode of the transfiguration, Jesus is revealed as equal and even superior to Moses and Elijah. Jerusalem is the place where prophets die (13:33); nevertheless, Jesus foretells his own death several times and sets his face toward Jerusalem (9:53). When he arrives, he weeps over what is going to happen to the city under the Romans, and he prophesies the destruction of the temple (21:5–6). And to the wayfarers on the road to Emmaus, he explains his death on the grounds that the prophets had declared that the Messiah must suffer and die (24:25–27).

Throughout Luke's narrative, Jesus appears also as a good example to be imitated. Even at the moment of his death, he shows himself to be the best example of his own teachings about love and forgiveness toward enemies (Luke 23:34), of outreach to marginal persons (23:42), and of trust in God (23:46). Luke features women more prominently in his narrative, and he assumes that they accompanied Jesus from Galilee to Jerusalem (8:2–3). The inner circle of disciples are the twelve apostles, and they provide the principles of continuity between the time of Jesus and the time of the church. While retaining the already-but-not-yet stance toward the kingdom of God, Luke shows in more detail how to deal with the apparent delay of Jesus' second coming, and prepares for what will be his second volume, the Acts of the Apostles.

**9. John emphasizes Jesus as the revealer and the revelation of God.** Put in final form late in the first century AD, perhaps at Ephesus, John's Gospel reflects the language and theology of a distinct movement in early Christianity known as the Johannine community (**Raymond E. Brown, 1979**). It had some early connection to John the son of Zebedee and the Beloved Disciple (perhaps they were the same person), but seems to have been the product of long periods of reflection on the significance of Jesus. After an introductory chapter, this Gospel treats in chapters 2 to 12 the public ministry of Jesus in Galilee and Judea. Because it features seven miracles on Jesus' part, this section is often called the Book of Signs. The remainder of the Gospel (chapters 13 to 21) consists of Jesus' Farewell Discourses at the Last Supper and the passion and resurrection narratives (**Francis J. Moloney**). Because it interprets Jesus' death and resurrection not as a defeat but as a great victory, that part is often called the Book of Glory.

The opening of John's Gospel (John 1:1–18) identifies Jesus as the Word of God. It claims that in the beginning the Word was with God and was God, and that the Word became flesh and lived among us. As the man from heaven, Jesus has come to reveal who God is and what God wants of us. The focus of Jesus' preaching is himself and his role as the revealer and revelation of God. There is little explicit mention of the kingdom of God, presumably because Jesus *embodies* the kingdom of God. His passion, death, resurrection, and exaltation taken as a single event constitute the "hour" of Jesus in which he fulfills his mission on earth and returns to his heavenly Father.

The disciples accompany Jesus during his public ministry and listen to his discourses. However, they frequently misunderstand him, and this provides the occasion for Jesus to go into greater depth. During the Farewell Discourses, he tells them how they might carry on the movement that he began, especially by keeping his commandments to believe and to love and by being open to the guidance of the Holy Spirit/Paraclete. The Mother of Jesus appears at the beginning of Jesus' public ministry (2:1–11) and at the cross (19:25–27). The Beloved Disciple serves as a model to be imitated and perhaps as a counterpoint to Peter. The opponents of Jesus are referred to as "the Jews" and "the world." Of all the Gospels, John places the most emphasis on the "already," or present, dimension of eschatology. For those who believe in Jesus as the Word of God, eternal life has already begun.

**10. *The so-called Apocryphal Gospels tell us more about second- and third-century Christianity than about Jesus and the New Testament.*** In the introduction to his Gospel, Luke claims to have investigated earlier sources in the process of producing his own "orderly account." We can be sure that these sources included Mark's Gospel and the Sayings Source Q. But were there others, and what were they? There is a lot of special material (L) in Luke's Gospel: the infancy narrative, the parables of the Good Samaritan and the Prodigal Son, and so on. Whether this material came from one source or several is hard to know. There is also a body of material known as the Agrapha, that is, sayings attributed to Jesus but not written in the four Gospels (e.g., the saying referred to in Acts 20:35).

There is a category of early Christian texts known as the Apocryphal Gospels (**J. Keith Elliott**). Many of them are associated with figures familiar from the canonical New Testament: *Gospel of Peter, Gospel of Judas, Gospel of Philip, Gospel of Thomas, Gospel of Mary, Infancy Gospel of Thomas, Protoevangelium of James*, and so on. Some of these texts have been available for many years, while others were among the Coptic documents found at Nag Hammadi in Egypt in the late 1940s.

The *Infancy Gospel of Thomas* purports to provide information about the childhood of Jesus. In it, Jesus the child prodigy makes sparrows out of clay that fly away, strikes other children dead, and instructs his teacher. This fantastic story is clearly a product of human imagination designed to entertain and to fill a gap in the canonical Gospels. The *Gospel of Thomas* is a collection of 114 sayings attributed to Jesus. Many of them are obviously gnostic in their language and thought, though some scholars have argued that, beneath the gnostic veneer, the collection may preserve earlier forms of some of Jesus' sayings than those found in the Synoptic Gospels. The recently published *Gospel of Judas*, while initially advertised as revealing important information about earliest Christianity, turned out to be a gnostic document in which Judas supposedly wants to help Jesus free himself from his fleshly body. The *Gospel of Peter* provides an account of the passion, death, and resurrection of Jesus that seems largely based on material from the canonical Gospels. It is most famous for its alleged description of the resurrection of Jesus (something not found in the canonical Gospels) in which two angels come down from heaven, roll away the stone from the entrance of Jesus' tomb, and escort him from the tomb to heaven "with a cross following them."

None of the Apocryphal Gospels matches the canonical Gospels in substance and theology, and many of them should not be called Gospels at all. They belong more to the history of Christianity in the second and third centuries than to New Testament study. They do, however, raise some interesting questions: Were they meant to be real history, imaginative exercises, or simple entertainments? Were they the products of individuals, fringe groups, or major movements? And how seriously are they to be taken today? Of course, the Apocryphal Gospels deserve to be edited, translated, and studied carefully for their theological and historical significance. However, it appears that we should not expect to learn much from them about Jesus and earliest Christianity.

***Concluding Comment***: While there is general recognition of the complexity of the process by which the four canonical Gospels came to be, there are still questions surrounding the reconstruction of the Sayings Source Q, the value of the sayings in the *Gospel of Thomas* and in other Apocryphal Gospels, and the Two-Source Theory as the solution to the Synoptic Problem. While there is general agreement that the Gospels should be read as originally speaking to a specific community such as Matthew's Jewish Christian community in Antioch, or the Johannine community, there is the historical question of how and when the Gospel's began to circulate among Christian communities all around the Mediterranean. There is also the theological question of the degree to which the Evangelists imagined themselves writing for all the churches or mainly for their own specific community. Finally, while the use of the new narrative-critical literary methods has greatly illumined the Gospels as literature, the fact that they prescind from historicity and indeed work best with fiction raises questions about interpreting the Gospels as historical documents.

# CHAPTER FIVE

# New Perspectives on Paul and Judaism

In the history of relations between Jews and Christians, the figure of Paul of Tarsus has been controversial and often divisive. Many Jews have regarded Paul as an apostate and as the real founder of the religion known as Christianity. Many Christians have celebrated Paul as the convert who showed that right relationship with God (justification) is through faith alone and as the one who has freed us from the burden of observing all the precepts of the Mosaic Law.

In recent years, however, biblical scholars, both Jews and Christians, have developed new and better ways of looking at Paul and his letters. They have tried to take much more seriously first-century Judaism as the proper context for understanding Paul's life and work, and to place Paul's preaching about the saving significance of Jesus' death and resurrection in its wider biblical framework. In academic circles, these developments have become an actual movement known as "the New Perspective on Paul." However, since not all the proponents agree on every matter, I prefer the more general term "new perspectives on Paul."

The new perspectives on Paul described here reflect the renewed scholarly interest in first-century Judaism inspired by the discovery of the Dead Sea Scrolls in the late 1940s, theological reflection on the tragic role of Christian theology and practice in the European Shoah, and the firm resolve expressed in Vatican II's *Nostra aetate* (1965) to rethink the church's relationship to the Jewish people in Pauline terms.

Here are ten key points to remember when approaching considering the new perspectives on Paul:

**1. Paul's work and writings must be interpreted in the context of first-century Judaism.** According to the New Testament, Paul was a person of several worlds: a Diaspora Jew raised in Tarsus, an orator and a writer trained in the conventions of Greek rhetoric, and a citizen of the Roman Empire. Without denying Paul's cosmopolitan credentials, the new perspective on Paul emphasizes his identity as a Jew living shortly before the destruction of the Second Temple in Jerusalem.

In Philippians 3:5–6, Paul lists his Jewish credentials: "circumcised on the eighth day, a member of the people of Israel, of the tribe of Benjamin, a Hebrew born of Hebrews; as to the law a Pharisee; as to zeal, a persecutor of the church; as to righteousness under the law, blameless." Likewise, in Galatians 1:14 he claims, "I advanced in Judaism beyond many among my people of the same age, for I was far more zealous for the traditions of ancestors."

Paul's Bible was the Greek version of the Jewish Scriptures (the Septuagint), what Christians call the Old Testament. His own letters, of course, are the earliest complete compositions in the New Testament, from the 50s of the first century CE. Like many other late–Second Temple Jews, Paul adopted the language and style of the Jewish Bible, and applied the various interpretive techniques commonly used in reading its texts. Besides their hundreds of allusions to, and echoes of, the Jewish Bible, his letters contain almost one hundred explicit quotations from it, roughly one-third of all the Old Testament quotations in the New Testament. The bulk of them are taken from the Pentateuch, Isaiah, and Psalms. They appear mainly in what are regarded as Paul's most important letters: Romans, 1 and 2 Corinthians, and Galatians. Paul's abundant use of the Jewish Scriptures in his most substantial letters indicates that for him and his first readers (mainly Gentile Christians), these texts continued to possess great authority.

However, Paul's experience of the risen Jesus on the road to Damascus became the ultimate authority for him, to the point that he would dismiss his impeccable credentials as a Jew as "loss" and even "rubbish" (Phil 3:7–8). That experience led Paul to regard Christ as the key to the correct interpretation of all the Jewish Scriptures. Such an approach has many parallels in Second Temple Judaism. As the pesharim and other Dead Sea Scrolls show, the Qumran people regarded their community's history and life together as providing the solution to the many puzzles and mysteries in the biblical prophecies and psalms (**Timothy H. Lim**). The Jewish apocalyptists behind the Book of Daniel, *4 Ezra*, and *2 Baruch* looked forward to the fulfillment of God's promises to his people in the near future. Likewise, the rabbis considered Israel's continuing existence as God's holy people to be the key to the Jewish Scriptures. In this context, Paul and other early Christians took Jesus of Nazareth as the key that unlocked the Scriptures of Israel.

At the heart of Paul's thoroughly biblical theology was God's promise to Abraham in Genesis 17 that he would become "the ancestor of a multitude of nations" (17:5). In the biblical narrative, God's covenant with Abraham was the divine response to the sin of Adam and Eve, Cain's murder of Abel, the sinfulness of the flood generation, and the arrogance of those who built the Tower of Babel (see Genesis 1 to 11). Paul regarded the death and resurrection of Jesus as the pivotal event in the history of salvation, whereby God's covenant relationship with Israel might be extended to all nations and God's promise to Abraham might be fulfilled as we all await the full coming of God's kingdom.

**2. Jews observed the law in the context of their covenant relationship with God ("covenantal nomism"); first-century Jews were not legalists per se.** The oppositions between Judaism (righteousness by works: legalism) and Christianity (righteousness by faith alone: love) are not well founded. In the Christian tradition, teachers and preachers have often labeled Jews as legalists and contrasted them with Christians who supposedly are guided only by faith and love. These stereotypes are not only untrue but have also been dangerous throughout history. One of the important new perspectives on Paul has been the effort at recovering the biblical framework of covenant and recognizing that the laws set down in the Torah are placed in the context of God's love expressed in creation, in his promises to the patriarchs, and in his liberation of Israel from slavery in Egypt. In this framework, observing the 613 precepts in the Torah represents the proper response of God's people to the covenant fidelity that God has so abundantly shown in its early history. This covenant framework is, at least ideally, what Jews through the centuries have embraced and acted upon. Their approach has been described as "covenantal nomism" (**E. P. Sanders, 1977**), that is, observing the Jewish Law (Torah in Hebrew, *nomos* in Greek) in the context of Israel's covenant relationship with God.

Paul's attitude toward the Jewish Law is ambiguous, to say the least. On the one hand, he claims that the law is "holy and just and good" (Rom 7:12), and that "we uphold the law" (Rom 3:31). On the other hand, Paul describes the law in Galatians 3:24–25 as a kind of disciplinarian or *paidagogos*, a slave who escorted children to school and provided guidance along the way. More controversial and problematic is Paul's depiction of the law as a malevolent power that specifies sins and so entices persons to commit them (Rom 7:7–25). In this way, Paul portrays the law as an ally of the powers of sin and death. He goes so far as to suggest in Galatians 3:19–20 that the law was given to Moses through the mediation of angels, a tradition found in other Jewish and early Christian texts.

Some representatives of the new perspective have argued that Paul was simply confused on this matter (notably **Heikki Räisänen**). Perhaps *ambiguous* is a better term.

Writing some twenty-five years after Jesus' death, Paul was necessarily creating some aspects of Christian theology as he went along. While we can sympathize with Paul's ambiguity, it is the merit of the new perspective on Paul to have recovered the authentic Jewish framework of covenantal nomism, and to have pointed out some apparent contradictions in Paul's statements about the Mosaic Law. While it may be possible to find some statements in ancient Jewish texts that sound like legalism, to dismiss Judaism as mere legalism is unfair and even slanderous.

***3. Paul's experience of the risen Christ trumped his past in Judaism, and yet he had no "guilty conscience" with regard to his past in Judaism.*** Like most New Testament writers and, indeed, most writers in the Greco-Roman world, Paul seldom provides much autobiographical information or insight into his personal feelings. However, in Galatians 1:13–17 and Philippians 3:2–16, Paul describes his own conversion, or call, in some detail. In both cases, he looks back on his life before his experience of the risen Christ with pride in his accomplishments in Judaism.

When reflecting on his attempt to persecute and destroy the early Christian movement, Paul observes that he had "advanced in Judaism beyond many among my people of the same age" (Gal 1:14). The implication is that he persecuted the Greek-speaking Jewish Christians out of the conviction that they had gone beyond the boundaries of traditional Judaism and that their movement had to be stopped. Likewise in Philippians 3, when listing his credentials as a Jew, Paul places in a climactic position the claim that he was "as to righteousness under the law, blameless" (3:6). Although Paul may have violated certain precepts along the way, in his own mind he regarded himself as blameless. The idea that Paul had a tender conscience stems largely from his anguished reflection in Romans 7 where he describes the human condition before and apart from Christ and employs first-person-singular language. But today that passage is generally seen as a meditation on the sorry state of humankind without Christ. The impression that Paul the Jew had a tender conscience was reinforced by the prominence of his two great interpreters, Augustine and Martin Luther, who struggled with their own tender consciences (**Krister Stendahl**).

If we accept Paul's own words at face value—that he had advanced in Judaism and was blameless with regard to the law—it seems that what changed Paul's mind and his life was his experience of the risen Jesus on the road to Damascus. In light of that experience, what had been the source of Paul's greatest pride—his blameless life in Judaism —paled by comparison to the point that it now appeared to be "loss" and even "rubbish" (Phil 3:8). What became much more important to him was "knowing Christ and the power of his resurrection and the sharing of his sufferings by becoming like him in his death, if somehow I may attain the resurrection from the dead" (Phil 3:10–11).

*4. Paul's "conversion" involved a "call." His conversion was from one form of Judaism (Pharisaic) to another (Christian). His call was to bring the gospel (the good news of Jesus Christ) to non-Jews (Gentiles).* When students of religion treat the topic of conversion, their prototype is often the case of Paul the apostle. Luke, the author of the Acts of the Apostles, describes Paul's conversion three times and in great detail (see Acts 9, 22, and 26). Paul himself describes it in less detail in Galatians 1 and Philippians 3. How and why Paul converted has been analyzed from many different perspectives—psychological, sociological, and so on. But none of these reductive explanations has been totally satisfying. And so we are left with Paul's own testimony that his experience of the risen Christ was so overpowering that it brought about remarkable changes in his worldview and activity.

Yet a careful reading of Paul's own testimony indicates that he continued to regard himself as a Jew who had once belonged to the Pharisaic Jewish movement and now belonged to the Christian Jewish movement. In other words, he moved from one form of Judaism to another (**Alan Segal**).

Despite the impression given in the Gospels and in much New Testament scholarship, the Pharisees were a progressive party within Judaism (**Anthony J. Saldarini, 2001**). They were eager to adapt the prescriptions of the Torah to the changing conditions of their time. They shared their wisdom in fellowship meals, extended the spirituality of Israel as a priestly people to lay folk, promoted beliefs in the resurrection of the dead and in postmortem rewards and punishments, and gathered the teachings of earlier sages. Among the several Jewish groups active in Jesus' time, Jesus seems to have stood closest to the Pharisees, at least to the extent of sharing an agenda with them

It has been observed that, although you can take Paul out of the Pharisees, you can't take the Pharisee out of Paul. Indeed, it is possible to detect lingering elements of Pharisaism in Paul's letters. Nevertheless, it seems that in Paul's mind he had shifted his allegiance from one form of Judaism to another as the result of his experience of the risen Christ.

Moreover, according to his own testimony, Paul's "conversion" involved a call or vocation to "proclaim him [Christ] among the Gentiles" (Gal 1:16). In describing his call, Paul alludes to the call of Jeremiah the prophet: "God, who had set me apart before I was born and called me through his grace..." (Gal 1:15; see Jer 1:5). As a result Paul interpreted his conversion as also a call to bring the good news about Jesus to non-Jews so that they too might become part of the people of God.

**5. Paul did not set out to found a new religion separate from Judaism. Rather, he regarded himself as a Jew and viewed Jesus as the fulfillment of God's promises to Israel.** In responding to the risen Christ's call to bring the gospel to non-Jews, Paul did not think that he was starting a new religion. Indeed, Paul did not invent the Christian mission to non-Jews. Rather, from the accounts in Acts 10 to 11, it appears that the Gentile mission began when certain non-Jews expressed their interest in becoming part of the Christian movement (**Martin Hengel** and **Anna Maria Schwemer**).

What quickly became a problem and a matter of great controversy were the conditions under which Gentiles might be accepted into the Christian community. From several of Paul's letters (Galatians, 2 Corinthians, and Philippians) it appears that some prominent Jewish Christians insisted that Gentiles had to become fully Jewish by undergoing circumcision and observing the precepts of the Torah. These Jewish Christians presumably suspected that Paul was in danger of starting a new religion and wanted to stop him.

Paul, however, was convinced that the success of the Gentile mission had revealed something more basic to Judaism—the fidelity of Abraham to God's covenantal promise that he would become the father of many nations—than even the Torah given to Moses on Mount Sinai. What mattered most to Paul was his conviction that Gentile Christians had received the Holy Spirit (see Gal 3:1–5) without undergoing circumcision and observing the Torah. Moreover, Paul viewed Jesus as the true offspring of Abraham (Gal 3:16) and as the pivotal figure in salvation history, whose saving death and resurrection had opened up a place for non-Jews in the people of God. Paul thought that what God was doing through Jesus was expanding the parameters of God's people rather than founding a new religion separate from Judaism.

According to Acts 15, the leaders of the early Christian movement (including Paul) met in Jerusalem and agreed on a compromise. According to their decree, non-Jews were to be accepted into the Christian community if they abstained "from what had been sacrificed to idols and from blood and from what is strangled and from fornication" (Acts 15:29). However, there is not much evidence that this decree was strictly enforced in early Christian circles or even that Paul insisted on it in guiding his Gentile Christian communities.

**6. Could non-Jews be part of the people of God? The major and most pressing concern in Paul's Letter to the Galatians and Letter to the Romans was not the theological principle of justification by faith but this ecclesiological/pastoral question.** Paul's Letter to the Galatians and his Letter to the Romans are generally regarded as his most significant theological statements. They provide the strongest support for the doctrine of justification by faith, which in many Christian circles is regarded as the core of Pauline theology and indeed of all Christian theology.

While admitting that justification is an important theme in these letters, proponents of the new perspective contend that these two letters are ultimately concerned with membership in the church. The major question they deal with is, How can non-Jews be part of the people of

God? In Galatians, Paul seeks to rebut the claims of rival Jewish Christian missionaries that Gentiles had to become fully Jewish. In Romans, he was trying to get Jewish Christians and Gentile Christians to look upon one another as equals before God.

Paul is best described as a pastoral theologian. He was not a professor writing books on general topics in the quiet of his office. Rather, Paul was a founder of Christian communities, and his letters were extensions of his pastoral ministry. In them, he sought to respond to pastoral crises and to answer questions that arose in his physical absence.

In the course of responding to the ecclesial problems facing the Galatian and Roman Christians, Paul developed the idea of justification by faith. It is a legal image and presupposes the setting of a trial. It imagines God as a judge who delivers a verdict in favor of one of the litigants and allows that litigant to start over with a clean slate. There are some echoes of the Jewish theology of the Day of Atonement. However, the Pauline version places its emphasis on the favor or grace displayed by God and on faith or fidelity as the proper response to the divine favor and fidelity.

Without dismissing the importance of justification, **N. T. Wright (2009)** insists that the concept must be placed in the wider context of God's covenant relationship with Abraham, the pivotal role played by Jesus in the history of salvation, the law-court image as the setting for both the divine decree of justification in the present and for the Last Judgment, and the opening up of God's people to all the nations through the Holy Spirit. In other words, justification must be viewed in its comprehensive biblical and covenantal theological framework.

**7. For Paul, the faith of Christ (that is, Jesus' fidelity to God) came before and provided the basis for our faith in**

73

**Christ (that is, Jesus as the object of our faith).** One of Paul's favorite Greek theological terms is *pistis*, which is usually translated as "faith." And one of his favorite uses of that word is with "Christ" or "Christ Jesus" in the genitive case **(Richard B. Hays).** A beginner in the study of New Testament Greek might naturally translate the phrase *pistis Iesou Christou* in Romans 3:22 as "the faith of Jesus Christ." In that context, it might refer to the trust and fidelity to God's covenant and plan that Jesus displayed during his earthly life, especially in accepting the cup of suffering in the passion narrative. Such trust and fidelity are graphically depicted in the Gethsemane episode in Mark 14:32–42. This interpretation takes the genitive case as subjective, that is, the fidelity possessed and demonstrated by Jesus.

However, in the English Bible tradition, it has become customary to interpret the noun in the genitive case as an objective genitive, that is, "faith *in* Christ." In this rendering, what is important is the faith displayed by those who believe in the saving significance of Jesus' death and resurrection. The idea of faith in Christ and the justification before God that it brings about has been (and still is) a pivotal doctrine in many forms of mainline and Evangelical Protestantism. It has always seemed to me, however, that this kind of faith is in danger of becoming a "work"—just the kind of "works righteousness" that the Protestant Reformers sought to combat.

It is worth noting that the *New Revised Standard Version of the Bible* (1989)—the most widely used English Bible and sponsored by the Protestant National Council of Churches in the USA—usually retains the traditional rendering ("faith in Christ") in the main text but in each case adds in a footnote the alternative ("the faith of Christ"). This practice is an invitation to readers to reflect on which translation—"the faith of Christ" (subjective genitive) or "faith in Christ" (objective genitive)—better fits the passage under consideration. At the very least, the new perspectives on Paul make us rethink what Paul believed about Jesus and how believers relate to God through him.

**8. Paul's reasoning moves from solution (Christ) to plight (all humankind before and apart from Christ was under the powers of sin, death, and the law).** This thesis picks up the problem described in number 2, about the Mosaic Law as a tool and ally of sin and death in Paul's Letter to the Romans. There he shows that all humankind, Gentiles and Jews alike, found themselves enslaved to sin and death. Paul rarely uses "Satan" language. Instead he prefers to personify sin, death, and the law as powers subjugating all humans. They function as a kind of unholy trinity, or gang of three, serving as the equivalent of the Prince of Darkness in the Jewish schema of a modified apocalyptic dualism glimpsed in the Dead Sea Scrolls (*Rule of the Community*, cols. 3–4).

According to Paul in Romans 1, the Gentiles failed to recognize the true God from creation itself, and their fundamental mistake about God led them into a downward spiral of sin. Likewise, the Jews, according to Romans 2:1—3:8, even though they had the law, failed to observe it properly. This bleak picture of humankind before and apart from Christ is reaffirmed in Paul's anthology of biblical quotations in Romans 3:10–18, placed under the heading "all, both Jews and Greeks, are under the power of sin" (3:9).

According to Paul, Jesus, especially in his death and resurrection, was the divinely appointed solution to the plight of humankind. The thesis of Paul's Letter to the Romans is that the gospel is "the power of God for salvation to everyone who has faith" (1:16). So convinced was Paul that Jesus was the solution that he seems to have portrayed the plight in the darkest way possible. This is why some proponents of the new perspectives describe Paul's reasoning as proceeding from solution to plight.

Which raises the question: Was Paul an optimist or a pessimist? In his analysis of all humankind as enslaved under sin, death, and the law, Paul was clearly a pessimist about what humans do on their own without God's help through Christ and the Holy Spirit. In his analysis of the coming of Christ and what it meant for the human condition, Paul may have overestimated at least the tangible results. Of course, Paul embraced the twofold character of Jewish eschatology ("this age" and "the age to come"). But he also believed that Christ has inaugurated the age to come and looked forward in hope to the fullness of God's kingdom.

**9. For Paul, "works of the law" were first and foremost the distinctive identity markers attached to Judaism: circumcision, Sabbath observance, and food and purity laws.** In much Christian teaching and preaching on Paul, there has been a tendency to caricature Judaism as a legalism, that is, the belief that one can earn one's salvation on the basis of good works and in particular by keeping the 613 commandments in the Torah. In the Reformation tradition, alleged Jewish legalism has often served as a not-very-subtle code for criticizing Catholicism and its teachings about merit accruing from good works.

In Galatians 3:2, an exasperated Paul asks the Gentile Christians whom he had brought to Christian faith, "Did you receive the Spirit by doing the works of the law or by believing what you heard?" Paul's real problem with the law was that it could not do what he believed Christ had done, that is, make possible right relationship with God (justification).

But what did Paul mean by the "works of the law?" Was it the 613 precepts in the Torah as they were counted by the rabbis? Or did Paul have something more specific in mind? According to some representatives of the new perspectives on

Paul, the "works of the law" were those practices that made Jews stand out in the Greco-Roman world and so had come to serve as identity markers for Jews: circumcision, Sabbath observance, and food and purity laws (**James D. G. Dunn, 2005**). These practices made Jews look foreign and mysterious to outsiders, and functioned as boundary markers within which Jews could celebrate what made them into a distinct people spread all over the Mediterranean world.

In writing to the Galatians, Paul does not refer much to Sabbath observance (although see 4:10). He does reprove Peter for his failure of nerve in refusing to eat with Gentile Christians and to regard them as his spiritual equals. Rather, he focuses more on the practice of circumcision as being unnecessary for Gentile Christians. He contends that what makes one a true child of Abraham is faith understood as trust in God's covenant and his unfolding plan for humankind (3:6–29). He suggests that circumcision for Gentile Christians is at best a matter of indifference (5:6), and he accuses his rival Jewish Christian missionaries of trying to gain control over Gentile Christians and to limit their freedom (6:13). He even goes so far as to wish (crudely) that those proponents of circumcision might castrate themselves (5:12).

**10. Paul looked forward to the salvation of "all Israel" (Rom 11:25–26).** In Romans 9–11, Paul tries to put together the three great entities in his vision of salvation history: Jewish Christians like himself, Gentiles who had embraced the good news about Jesus, and those fellow Jews who had not accepted the gospel. That this was a matter of great personal significance to Paul is clear from the passionate introduction (9:1–5) to his long meditation on the topic. There he rehearses Israel's prerogatives in salvation history ("the adoption, the glory, the covenants"), and claims that he was willing to be cut off from Christ (the most important thing in his life) if only his fellow Jews would accept the gospel.

The simplest way to explain Paul's long and complicated train of thought in Romans 9–11 is to use his own analogy of the olive tree in 11:17–24. The olive tree is occasionally used as a biblical symbol for Israel as the people of God. Jewish Christians like himself constitute the root of the olive tree. Paul could not envision the church without its roots in historical Israel. Gentile Christians are compared to the branches of a wild olive tree that have been grafted on to the cultivated olive tree. Non-Christian Jews are described as branches that have been broken off from the olive tree. Here Paul reminds Gentile Christians that if God could graft branches from the wild olive tree (Gentile Christians) on to the cultivated olive tree, how much easier will it be for God to graft back the natural branches (other Jews) on to their own olive tree!

In what can be called his *eureka* moment, Paul states what he regarded as the solution to the mystery of God's plan for Israel's salvation. He writes in Romans 11:25–26: "I want you to understand this mystery: a hardening has come upon part of Israel, until the full number of Gentiles has come in. And so all Israel will be saved." Here Paul takes over the biblical motif of the divine hardening of Israel from Isaiah 6:9–10 and the Jewish apocalyptic motif of a divine quota of those to be saved. Thus, Paul views the rejection of the gospel by many Jews and its acceptance by a surprising number of Gentiles providentially in accord with the divine plan for all Israel's salvation (as he had made clear already in Romans 11:1–16).

Paul's grand conclusion in Roman 11:26 is this: "And so all Israel will be saved." Unfortunately, Paul fails to tell us exactly who "all Israel" is (each and every Jew, Israel taken as a collective, or the church?); when it will be saved (in history, or at the end of time?); and how it will be saved (through some experience of Christ as he had had, through missionary activity, or through a separate way designed by God?). While we must be grateful for what Paul tells us, we also wish that he had answered those three important questions.

***Concluding Comment***: Taken together, these new perspectives place Paul more fully within the context of first-century Judaism. Thus, we can see more clearly the power of Paul's conversion/call and the issues that shaped and often frustrated his apostolic activity. Most of the opposition to the new perspectives on Paul has come from conservative Protestant scholars (**Donald A. Carson et al.; Seyoon Kim**). For many of them, the Reformation heritage of *sola scriptura* and justification by faith alone is at stake. Their major concern has been the dilution of Paul the theologian into the historical Paul—the first-century Mediterranean Jewish apostle of Christian Judaism. As in the case of the quest for the historical Jesus, again we encounter the conflicts between historical particularity and abiding significance, between history and theology, and between justification by faith alone and mystical experience or salvation history as the center of Paul's theology and apostolic activity.

I must also note here that there is a *newer* "new perspective on Paul," and that it comes from a very unlikely source: European philosophers, most of them non-Christians and even nontheists, who have taken a lively interest in Paul's writings. As philosophers, they show little interest in Paul's historical context and are primarily concerned with his ideas. For those who are not familiar with current Continental European philosophy, their interpretations of Paul are very difficult to understand.

# CHAPTER SIX

# Christians in the Roman Empire

In recent years, New Testament scholars have taken more seriously than ever the fact that Christianity took shape in the Roman Empire. Some even seem to find political allusions and concerns almost everywhere, and thus run the risk of reducing the New Testament into a purely political document. But at least the current academic fascination with the Roman Empire as the political context of the New Testament can serve as a healthy corrective to the earlier tradition of the a-historical and exclusively theological reading of these texts.

This chapter deals mainly with what happened to the early Christian movement after Easter, and puts forth ten thesis statements to show how the Acts of the Apostles, the Epistles, and the Book of Revelation are best understood in the context of the Roman Empire.

*1. The Roman Empire was the larger context in which Jesus lived and the early church grew.* In the second century BC, the Jewish leaders known as the Maccabees entered into an alliance with the Romans. The Jews sought a powerful ally, and the Romans sought a foothold in the eastern Mediterranean. By 60 BC, Roman control over Palestine had increased greatly, and eventually the Herod family emerged as Rome's "client kings" in the areas. Thus, when Jesus was born, Herod the Great was ruler (37–4 BC) over the land of Israel; and when he died, his son Herod Antipas ruled in

Galilee and Pontius Pilate was the Roman prefect, or governor, of Judea from AD 26 to 36.

Rome changed from being a republic to being an empire under Caesar Augustus, who ruled from 40 BC to AD 14. He was in power when Jesus was born (Luke 2:1). Tiberius (AD 14–37) was the emperor when John the Baptist and Jesus came on the scene (Luke 3:1), and when both died. He was followed by the mad Gaius Caligula (AD 37–41), the crafty Claudius (41–54), and dissolute Nero (54–68), who was famous for blaming the Christians for the great fire of Rome (AD 64). Both Vespasian (69–79) and his son Titus (79–81) made their mark by putting down the Jewish rebellion and destroying Jerusalem and its temple in AD 70. Titus's brother Domitian (81–96) was the emperor when the Book of Revelation was written, in which he is identified as the "beast from the sea."

The existence of the Roman Empire did much to facilitate the spread of early Christianity. As the movement made its way out of Palestine, it flourished especially in the urban centers (**Wayne A. Meeks**): Antioch, Ephesus, Corinth, Athens, and Rome. The development of a relatively good road system throughout the empire and the defeat of the pirates roaming the Mediterranean Sea made travel between cities relatively safe. The general use of Greek (not Latin) as a common language helps explain why all the New Testament books were composed in Greek. The presence of Jewish communities in most of the big cities of the empire gave Jewish Christian missionaries like Paul an entry point for their missionary activity. Paul himself grew up in Tarsus in Cilicia and very likely had both a Jewish education as well as a Greco-Roman rhetorical education in which he was exposed to the works of classical writers and which served him well as he wrote his own letters.

*2. There is no single attitude toward the Roman Empire in the New Testament.* All the books of the New

Testament were written in the shadow of the Roman Empire. But they were composed in different places over a period of fifty years or more (**Walter E. Pilgrim**). There is much in the Gospels to justify a political reading of Jesus' life and work. In the one episode in which Jesus is directly confronted and asked to put forward his views on the Roman Empire, he admits the obligation to pay taxes to Caesar but insists that fulfilling one's obligations to God is even more important (Mark 12:13–17). However, much of what Jesus said and did could be (and apparently was) interpreted as a threat to the Roman Empire. The focus of his teaching was "the kingdom of God." If God is king, then presumably Caesar is not. Along the way, Jesus drew large crowds, which was always a threat to both the Jewish and the Roman authorities. He began the last week of his life with a triumphal "royal" entrance into Jerusalem and a symbolic action expressing his sovereignty over the temple. He was condemned under the Roman prefect Pontius Pilate. And he was executed by crucifixion—a punishment generally reserved for political rebels and slaves.

In the Epistles, we get a different picture. In Romans 13:1–7, Paul seems to envision an ideal Roman Empire. He claims that the governing (Roman) authorities have been instituted by God, and urges cooperation with them and compliance with their (just) demands for various taxes. Whether Paul was serious or was simply awaiting the imminent coming of God's kingdom in its fullness (see 13:11–14) is much debated. In what's known as the Pastoral Epistles (1 and 2 Timothy and Titus), Christians are urged to pray "for kings and those in high positions, so that we may lead a quiet and peaceable life in all godliness and dignity" (1 Tim 2:2). The idea is that cooperation with the empire (in its ideal state) would enable Christians to settle down and practice their religion without external interference. This same cooperative approach is present in 1 Peter, where Gentile Christians are urged to accept the authority of the emperor and governors, and even to "honor the emperor" (2:13–14, 17).

Still another approach appears in the Book of Revelation. The problem there seems to have been the zeal of a local political and/or religious official in western Asia Minor in promoting the cult of the Roman emperor as a god and the goddess Roma as a symbol of the empire. The official was naturally expecting Christians to participate in this form of civic religion. However, such action was contrary to their belief that the risen Jesus was the real "Lord and God," not the emperor Domitian. Thus, in chapters 12 and 13, John develops the notion of an "unholy" trinity consisting of the great red dragon (Satan), the beast from the sea (the emperor), and the beast from the land (the local political/religious official). In chapters 17 and 18, he portrays Rome as "the great whore" (17:1), and takes delight in foreseeing the fall of the Roman Empire and all its political and economic clients. The issue was the attempt on the part of the local official to make Christians do things that were against their conscience. Revelation deals not with the ideal Roman Empire but rather with the (too-often) real Roman Empire.

**3. *The Acts of the Apostles can be a valuable resource in understanding the spread of early Christianity in the Roman Empire.*** Acts is the sequel to Gospel of Luke (**Luke Timothy Johnson, 1992**). Just as in the Gospel Luke sought to write an "orderly account" of Jesus' birth, public ministry, and passion and resurrection, so in Acts he intends to provide an "orderly account" of the spread of the early Christian movement from Jerusalem to Rome ("the ends of the earth," as Acts 1:8 puts it).

Luke's sequel begins with the narratives of Jesus' ascension and the descent of the Holy Spirit at Pentecost, and considers the evangelizing efforts of the apostles in Jerusalem and the expansion of their mission to Samaria and Judea (chapters 1 to 8). Next it describes in chapter 9 (and again in 22 and 26) the conversion of Paul, the onetime persecutor, into the one chosen by God to bring the gospel to the Gentiles. In 10:1—11:18, the Roman centurion Cornelius, a Gentile, becomes a Christian under the guidance of Peter, who himself comes to realize that all creatures are clean and so Gentiles need not follow the Jewish food laws. The decision that Gentiles may be admitted into the church without becoming Jews—and so without taking on the obligations of the Torah—is ratified at the Council of Jerusalem in Acts 15. Meanwhile, Paul and Barnabas are commissioned by the church at Antioch to spread the gospel to various cities in Asia Minor (present-day Turkey and Greece).

It has become customary to divide Paul's missionary activities as recounted by Luke into three "journeys": Acts 13:1—14:28; 15:41—18:22; and 18:23—20:38. Paul's usual strategy on entering a city is to go to the local synagogue (where he usually receives a mixed reception) and then to turn to the Gentiles, where he has great success. Except for chapter 17, throughout Acts the apostles including Paul all seem to give a similar kind of speech, showing how the Jewish Scriptures have been fulfilled in Jesus, invoking the testimony of John the Baptist, highlighting Jesus' death and resurrection, and urging the listeners to believe and be baptized. When Paul goes to Jerusalem, ostensibly to bring the proceeds of the collection to the church leaders there, he is arrested, undergoes various hearings and trials, and is finally sent to Rome to be tried as a Roman citizen. There, while under some kind of house arrest, Paul continues his mission of "proclaiming the kingdom of God and teaching about the Lord Jesus Christ with all boldness and without hindrance" (28:31). There the Book of Acts breaks off. We learn nothing more about Paul's plans for a mission to Spain (see Rom 15:24) or about his martyrdom at

Rome. Did Luke plan a third volume? Was he somehow impeded from finishing his story?

Acts can be a valuable resource in understanding the spread of early Christianity throughout the Roman Empire. There can be no doubt that it contains much important and reliable historical information. However, there is also no doubt that Acts is made up of some very good and colorful stories. That is one of the critical problems regarding Acts: How does one discern between story and history? Moreover, while Luke surely had access to many different sources, his rather narrow goal is to recount how the gospel traveled westward from Jerusalem to Rome. We learn nothing about how it traveled eastward or to Egypt in the south. Also Luke is very much interested in developing the parallelism between Jesus and the apostles, based obviously on his concern with Jesus as an example. Finally, the fact that all the apostles say virtually the same things indicates that Luke himself had a very clear concept of what early Christian preaching (*kerygma*) was and should be. If readers keep these cautions in mind, Acts can be a very good resource for understanding the spread of early Christianity throughout the Roman Empire.

**4. Paul's Letter to the Galatians and his Letter to the Romans explain why the church could and should be made up of both Jews and Gentiles.** Some of this material has already been covered in the chapter on Paul and Judaism. Also, in the previous thesis, we saw a rather smooth acceptance of the Gentile Cornelius into the Christian movement due to Peter's revelation about the purity laws and the official acceptance of this policy at the Council of Jerusalem. However, a careful reading of Paul's letters shows that this issue was a major one and that its resolution was not nearly as smooth as Luke suggests.

From several of Paul's letters (Galatians, Philippians, 2 Corinthians, and Romans), it appears that Paul was constantly shadowed and criticized by other Jewish Christian missionaries, who insisted that in order to become part of the Christian movement, Gentiles would first have to become Jews, that is, undergo circumcision, observe the Sabbath rest, and obey the food and purity laws. Paul objected to this approach because, in his own experience as an apostle, he had become convinced that certain Gentiles had already received the Holy Spirit apart from the Jewish law. Therefore, Gentiles did not need to become Jews (Gal 3:1–5). He was convinced that Christ through his death and resurrection had achieved what the Jewish law could not bring about: right relationship with God (justification, reconciliation, salvation, and so on).

In his Letter to the Galatians (**Frank J. Matera, 1992**), Paul tries to combat the charge made by other Jewish Christian missionaries that Paul had misled the Galatians by not insisting that they be circumcised. He does so by appealing to his own experience and to various biblical and theological arguments, and he warns the Galatians they should not allow his opponents or anyone else to infringe upon their newfound Christian freedom: "For freedom Christ has set us free. Stand firm, therefore, and do not submit again to a yoke of slavery" (Gal 5:1).

Writing to the Romans in the late 50s (**Brendan Byrne**), Paul seeks to explain to a mixed community of Jewish and Gentile Christians the significance of the good news about Jesus for all humans equally. He first argues that all people need the definitive revelation of God's covenant fidelity in Christ. Next he shows with reference to Abraham that faith in God's promises is the key to right relationship with God, and that Christ has made possible for all freedom from the power of sin, death, and the law, and freedom for life in the Holy Spirit. Then in Romans 9–11, Paul explains that Jewish Christians like himself are the root of the olive tree (Israel), that Gentile Christians have been grafted onto the olive tree, and that in the end God can and will restore non-Christian Jews back onto the olive tree on the grounds that "a hardening has come upon part of Israel, until the full number of Gentiles has come in. And so all Israel will be saved" (Rom 11:25–26). In the meantime, Jewish Christians and Gentile Christian stand as equals before God, and the presence of both groups is essential to the church.

**5. The Letter of James and the Gospel of Matthew reflect the Jewish Christian voice in the Roman Empire.** The "Letter" of James (**Patrick Hartin**) is really a Jewish wisdom instruction, like those found in Proverbs 1–9 and 22–24, and in the Book of Sirach. It treats many different topics without much of a visible structure. There are only two references to Jesus (James 1:1 and 2:1), and these are quite formulaic ("Lord Jesus Christ"). There are, however, several sayings that are paralleled in Matthew's Gospel (e.g., "do not swear," in 5:12; compare Matt 5:33–37).

The author of the letter identifies himself as "James." If this was the so-called brother of the Lord, then the text might be very early because we know that James was martyred in Jerusalem in AD 62. If, as is more likely, it was written in James's name, it was probably composed around AD 85 or later. In the canon of the New Testament, it is most famous for its "correction" of a version of the Pauline doctrine of justification by faith. James insists on both faith and works (2:14–26), although Paul himself might have agreed ("what counts is faith working through love," Gal 5:6).

There is little in the Letter of James that is specific to life in the Roman Empire, beyond the general applicability of its wise teachings. However, its emphasis on being "doers of the word" (1:22), definition of religion as caring for orphans and widows (1:27), and concern with keeping the Jewish law (2:10–13) indicates a form of early Christianity that prized its

Jewish roots and tried to stay in greater continuity with them than was the case in the Gentile Pauline communities.

In teaching about avoiding discrimination and insisting on social justice, James would surely have run into tension with the social and economic values of the Roman Empire. In 2:1–7, he argues that whoever comes into the Christian assembly, whether rich or poor, should be treated equally. Indeed, preference should be given to the poor, and in 5:1–6, he bitterly criticizes the rich in society. He warns them about the fleeting character of earthly riches, and accuses them of cheating their employees, being obsessed with their own luxury, and murdering those who resist them.

Matthew's Gospel (**Daniel J. Harrington, 1991**) was treated in chapter 4. But in this context of the Roman Empire, it deserves notice as another representative of Jewish Christianity. It seems to have been written for a largely Jewish Christian community around AD 85, perhaps at Antioch in Syria. It emphasizes the fulfillment of the Jewish Scriptures in Jesus, presents him as the authoritative Jewish teacher, and regards the community gathered around Jesus as the heir to the heritage of Israel after Jerusalem and its temple had been destroyed. Its occasion was in part the crisis facing all Jews about the future of that heritage after the events of AD 70. However, this is a Jewish Christianity that was ultimately open to the inclusion of Gentiles (**Anthony J. Saldarini, 1994**). Indeed, the Gospel ends with Jesus' command to "make disciples of all nations" (Matt 28:19).

**6. *Hebrews illustrates what it was like to be a Jewish Christian in the Roman Empire.*** Hebrews is not a letter, nor was it written for Hebrews, nor was Paul its author (**Alan C. Mitchell**). It seems to be basically a Christian sermon in written form. Only the final few verses at the end might identify it as a letter. It was composed mainly for Jewish Christians, not for Jews in general. And its literary style and theology are quite different from Paul's. While we do not know the author's name, we can be sure that it was not Paul. Its goal is to encourage Jewish Christians to remain faithful to their new form of Christian Judaism, and not revert to the kind of traditional Judaism from which they came. Whether it was written before or after the destruction of the Jerusalem temple in AD 70 remains a matter of dispute among scholars. It may well have been addressed to a Jewish Christian community in Rome.

As a good sermon, Hebrews interweaves biblical exposition and exhortation. In the first part (1:1—4:13) the author seeks to show by reference to various biblical texts that Jesus is superior to the angels, is the Son of Man referred to in Psalm 8, and is superior to Moses. The author's message to his Jewish Christian readers is that Christ is the key to the Jewish Scriptures. In the second part of Hebrews (4:14—10:18), he interprets Jesus' death as the perfect (in the sense of effective) sacrifice for sins and Jesus himself as the great high priest who willing offered himself as a sacrifice. In doing this, the author creates an older priesthood to which Christ belongs, that of Melchizedek (see Gen 14 and Ps 110), a priesthood superior to the Levitical priesthood that manned the Jerusalem temple. The message for Jewish Christians is that now, with the one perfect sacrifice of Christ, there is no longer need for the temple priesthood and the temple sacrifices. The final part of Hebrews (10:19—13:25) is a call for Jewish Christians to persevere in their new faith even if it means suffering social ostracism and death (10:32–34; 12:4). In the midst of their trials, they are urged to look to "Jesus the pioneer and perfecter of our faith" (12:2).

*7. First Peter illustrates what it was like to be a Gentile Christian in the Roman Empire.* Many New Testament scholars today regard 1 Peter (**Donald Senior**) as written not directly by the apostle but rather as originating in a Peter circle at Rome around AD 80. It is a circular letter addressed to Christians in various communities in the northern part of Asia Minor (present-day Turkey). Several expressions indicate that before their conversions these people were Gentiles (1:14; 1:18; 2:10; and so on), and not Jews. Nevertheless, after their conversion their identity as members of God's people was expressed in terms of ancient Israel's dignity at Mount Sinai: "But you are a chosen race, a royal priesthood, a holy nation, God's own people" (2:9; see Exod 19:6).

Several passages in 1 Peter suggest that the addressees once regarded themselves as "aliens and exiles" in the context of ancient Israel's status as God's special people: "during the time of your exile...ransomed from the futile ways inherited from your ancestors" (1:17–18). While this language may describe their "spiritual" exile, it is also possible that these people were, in fact, migrant workers moving from place to place in northern Asia Minor (**John H. Elliott**). In either case, their newfound faith gave them a new identity (Christians), a new community (the church), and a new home ("a home for the homeless").

The new identity is associated with the baptismal language that predominates in the text. In fact, some scholars have suggested that the letter as a whole is based on a baptismal homily or catechesis. In the salutation that opens the letter, the addressees are said to "have been chosen and destined by God the Father and sanctified by the Spirit to be obedient to Jesus Christ and to be sprinkled with his blood" (1:2). In the benediction that follows in 1:3–9, they are urged to bless God for their "new birth" (in baptism), which has given them the hope of sharing in Jesus' resurrection and eternal life. It also assures them that they will face suffering, but counsels them to regard it as a test or trial to be accepted and overcome. It concludes by assuring them that because they love and believe in Jesus, they will attain the salvation of their souls when the fullness of God's kingdom is revealed.

In the introduction to the ethical instructions in 2:11–12, they are addressed not only as "aliens and exiles" but also as members of God's people in Christ; the letter urges, "Conduct yourselves honorably among the Gentiles." While they are counseled to be good subjects of the Roman Empire and they are to give outsiders a good example appropriate to their own new faith, their new way of life also means that they now act in ways different from how they did formerly and from how their families, friends, and neighbors may still act. For that, they suffer at least a kind of social ostracism (4:3–4) or perhaps even worse ("the fiery ordeal," 5:12). In their suffering, however, they are to follow the example of Christ the Suffering Servant of Isaiah 53 (2:21–25; 4:13–19).

**8. Paul's First Letter to the Corinthians illustrates some of the problems facing Gentile Christians.** Corinth was a port city in southern Greece, at the nexus between east and west in the Mediterranean Sea. It was destroyed in 146 BC and refounded in 44 BC under Julius Caesar. Christianity was brought to Corinth by Paul. While he may have been able to establish a small nucleus of Jewish Christians there, the large majority by far were Gentile Christians. Eventually, Paul moved on in his missionary activity and ended up in Ephesus. There he received reports from members of his team about problems that had arisen in Corinth in his absence. He also seems to have received a letter from the Corinthians themselves, asking for his advice on how to deal with those problems and others.

People often imagine earliest Christianity as a "golden age." Far from it! Those who had become Christians may well have had some exposure to Judaism. But trying to absorb the Jewish Scriptures (to which Paul and others often appealed), and figuring out what attitudes and actions were then appropriate to their new life as Christians, were not easy tasks. But Paul is best described as a pastoral theologian. His letters were not so much academic tracts as they were vehicles for him to deal theologically with the problems that had emerged in his physical absence. In 1 Corinthians, we see Paul the pastoral theologian at work (**Raymond F. Collins**).

The first problem concerned factions within the Christian community (chapters 1 to 4). It seems that among the Corinthian Christians, there was rivalry based on the one by whom they had been baptized. Underlying this issue was a competition regarding who had the best wisdom and the best spiritual gifts. Paul responds by pointing to the mystery of the cross as the only wisdom that really counts (1:18–25), and by reminding them that the various apostles are all instruments of God in building up the body of Christ (3:5–17). In chapters 5 and 6, he deals in turn with incest between a member and his father's wife, associating with immoral persons, and lawsuits between members of the community being held in civil courts.

With chapter 7, Paul begins to take up the list of questions from the Corinthians. The first question concerns whether Christians should marry and engage in sexual relations. While holding up celibacy for the sake of God's kingdom as superior, he urges discernment to discover which state of life is most appropriate for the individuals concerned. In chapters 8 to 10, he treats the problems caused by meat having been sacrificed in pagan temples and then sold at the local markets. While he personally agrees with those who would permit Christians to eat such food on the grounds that the pagan gods are not really gods at all, he insists that all members of the community work out a pastoral solution that will also respect the scruples of those who think otherwise.

In chapter 11, he deals with the role of women in the Christian assembly and with order at the celebration of the Lord's Supper. While affirming that women can and should pray and prophesy at the assembly, he insists that women should look like women and men should look like men. With regard to the Lord's Supper, he objects to allowing social and economic differences being too prominent and thus distracting from the meaning of the Eucharist. In chapters 12 to 14, he considers divisions in the assembly caused by the spiritual gifts, especially speaking in tongues. Paul insists that "to each one is given the manifestation of the Spirit for the common good" (12:7), and places speaking in tongues at the bottom of his list. Finally, he responds to those who deny the resurrection by reflecting on its centrality in Christian faith from the beginning and by describing the resurrected body as a "spiritual" body, that is, totally empowered by the Holy Spirit.

**9. The later Pauline letters illustrate a social coming-to-terms with the Roman Empire.** Among New Testament scholars today, it is generally recognized that the Pastoral Epistles, Colossians, and Ephesians were written in Paul's name by students and admirers in the latter years of the first century, that is, after Paul's death. They seek to carry on the Pauline tradition, develop further some of Paul's theological ideas, and adapt Paul's teachings to new historical circumstances. One new circumstance was the phenomenon of the church settling down within the context of the Roman Empire.

Taking 1 Timothy as a representative of the Pastorals (**Benjamin Fiore**), we can see this development in the call to pray for kings and those in high positions (2:2); the emphasis on the importance of external respectability in society; the prominence of stable local leaders (bishops, deacons, and elders) within the community; the image of the church as the household of God (3:15); and the similarities in the ethical advice with that given by Greco-Roman moralists. This development is most clearly seen in attitudes toward women. Whereas women played important roles in the Jesus movement and in Paul's apostolic team, in these documents there is a reversion to the status that most women had in the Roman Empire.

Thus, 1 Timothy 2:8–15 presents directives about modesty in women's clothing, commands that "a woman learn in silence with full submission," blames Eve for the original sin, and observes that women will be saved through childbearing. Most (in)famous of all is the statement attributed to Paul: "I permit no woman to teach or have authority over a man; she is to keep silent" (2:12). On the other hand, much attention is given in 5:3–16 to systematic community support for widows who have no other means of security.

Of course, 1 Timothy contains brief summaries of faith (2:5–6; 3:16) that are precious indications of what early Christians believed about Jesus. Likewise, the Letter to the Colossians and the Letter to the Ephesians (**Margaret Y. MacDonald**) are full of good theology about Christ the Wisdom of God; the church as the body of Christ with Christ as its head; the unity of Jews and Gentiles in Christ; and Christ as the husband of the church. But they are also well known for what are called the household codes in Colossians 3:18—4:1 and Ephesians 5:21—6:9. These texts are instructions about the roles and obligations of the various members of a household: husband and wife, parents and children, and masters and slaves. This literary form is at least as old as Aristotle, and served to define the structure of the family in ancient Greece and in the Roman Empire. In Colossians, the hierarchical structure is softened by insistence that in the Christian household all human relationships are now "in the Lord," and by an emphasis on the mutual character of the obligations. In Ephesians, the author is really less interested in relationships in the human household (which he takes for granted) and much more interested in developing the analogy of the husband-wife relationship as a way of thinking about the relationship between Christ and the church.

**10. Paul's Letter to Philemon illustrates some of the sociopolitical tensions between the Roman Empire and the Christian movement.** Along with 2 John, 3 John, and Jude, the Letter to Philemon (**Judith M. Ryan**) is among the shortest documents in the New Testament. It is only one chapter. Surely by Paul himself, it gives a glimpse of life within a Christian household and the problems it faced with regard to the Roman Empire.

Paul had brought Philemon to Christian faith. One of the members of his household was a slave named Onesimus, who apparently had run away and eventually sought refuge with Paul in prison at Ephesus and there became a Christian. Paul's purpose in writing to Philemon was to urge him to take back Onesimus into his household without recrimination.

Living most likely in Colossae, Philemon customarily opened his (relatively large) house to the local Christian community. The early Christians had no temples (because they did not perform material sacrifices) or church buildings (those came later). Rather, they met in private households for fellowship and the Lord's Supper. Paul addressed his letter not only to Philemon, Apphia (perhaps his wife), and Archippus, but also to "the church in your house." It seems likely that Paul expected his letter to be read publicly before the whole community, thus putting pressure on Philemon to comply with his request.

Paul's request was that Philemon take Onesimus back "no longer as a slave but much more than a slave, a beloved brother" (v. 16). Slavery was a familiar institution in the Roman Empire and in many ways the foundation of its economy. The penalties imposed on runaway slaves were very serious. At the very least, Paul is asking Philemon to look upon his slave Onesimus as a brother in Christ and so as his equal, something that would have been very difficult and even offensive to a slave owner.

Paul may also be suggesting that Philemon should set Onesimus free, when he promises to repay Philemon for any harm Onesimus had done (probably in financial dealings) and expresses confidence that Philemon "will do even more than I say" (v. 21). What is that "even more"? If he means manumitting Onesimus, he threatens Philemon's reputation among his social peers (other slave owners) and his own economic stability. What if suddenly all the slaves in his household (and any other Christian household) became Christians, and demanded their freedom? In his short letter, Paul used all kinds of rhetorical devices to put pressure on Philemon. We do not know how the story turned out. But considering Philemon's social and economic problems allows us to view some of the dilemmas that early Christians faced in the Roman Empire.

**Concluding Comment**: Reading Acts and the Epistles in the context of the early Christian movement within the Roman Empire is not only sound historically but also illuminating theologically. However, some cautions are in order. Reducing the New Testament to a political codebook involves a category mistake of the highest order. The materials used in the social description of early Christians are often fragmentary and distant in time and place, and often cannot bear the weight imposed on them. The social-scientific concepts and methods developed in very different cultures and imposed on the New Testament may not fit well in the first century and can sometimes seem forced when the attempt is made to do so. And much of the support for the "empire" studies approach seems textually thin, apart from Revelation. There are surely anti–Roman Empire elements in the other texts. But how much is hard to discern, since there is ambiguity and their writers had to be careful lest their works might fall into hostile hands.

# Epilogue

In this book I have treated what I regard as six major developments in New Testament studies since Vatican II. The selection is admittedly subjective. Some readers may find my discussion a threat to long-held assumptions, while others may dismiss it as conservative and outdated. What it is, is a selective and concise summary of New Testament studies over the past fifty years by an aging Catholic biblical scholar who is an American Jesuit priest trained in biblical criticism and theology.

My starting point was Vatican II's 1965 document on divine revelation (*Dei verbum*), the most complete and authoritative statement on the Bible and its interpretation ever issued by the Catholic Church. A summary of its content showed how it provides a framework for understanding the nature of the Bible in Catholic thinking, opens up the possibilities and problems encountered in interpreting biblical texts, and encourages the application of various methods (old and new) in doing so.

Although the Qumran scrolls were discovered in 1947, the slow pace of their publication resulted in their continuing prominence and increased their importance in stimulating research on early Judaism. This scholarship in turn has enriched and changed our perceptions about Jews and Judaism in Jesus' time. While the scrolls never mention Jesus, they (and related literature) certainly help us to know better what was "in the air" and to discern what was distinctive about Jesus and the movement he began.

The so-called Third Quest has restored Jesus to his Jewish roots and his place within Judaism, while illustrating once more the difficulties involved in trying to write a biography of Jesus. Whatever else this quest has achieved, it has at least enabled us to recognize better how Jesus was perceived by his Jewish contemporaries, the centrality of the reign of God in his life and teachings, and who bears ultimate responsibility for his execution.

The renewed effort to describe in what sense the Evangelists may be regarded as authors has also clarified the complex process by which our four Gospels came into being. The Evangelists have emerged as both transmitters and interpreters of tradition. In their work as authors, they have produced four distinct portraits of Jesus. In shaping their material, they have highlighted different aspects of Jesus: suffering Messiah (Mark), teacher (Matthew), prophet and exemplar (Luke), and revealer and revelation of God (John).

The new perspectives on Paul and Judaism grew out of the general reassessment of Second Temple Judaism that was inspired by the discovery of the Qumran scrolls. While in some eyes Paul remained an apostate from Judaism and the founder of Christianity, it now appears that, in bringing the good news of Jesus Christ to non-Jews, Paul thought of himself as bearing witness to the fullness of Judaism. In its statement on the relationship of the Catholic Church to the Jewish people in *Nostra aetate* 4, Vatican II made extensive use of Paul's ideas expressed in Romans 9–11.

Finally, the renewal of interest in the Roman Empire as the historical setting for the New Testament has made scholars more aware of the proverbial "elephant in the room." It has shown that there is a wide variety of statements in the New Testament about the church's relationship to the Roman

Empire. It has also made us more sensitive to the process by which the small Jewish sect of Jesus' followers developed into what became a world religion, while managing to find a home within the Roman Empire.

In my view, *Dei verbum* is one of the great successes of Vatican II. It gave Catholics the authorization to pursue biblical study in its fullness, a framework for proceeding that honors both the historical and the spiritual dimensions of biblical texts, and the goal of making the Bible the "soul" of Christian theology and pastoral life.

The aim of this book has been to present my portrait of what has happened in New Testament studies over the past fifty years. What may happen in the future, I have tried to indicate in the "Concluding Comment" at the end of each chapter.

And so I end with the words of one of my favorite biblical authors, who in 2 Maccabees 15:38 wrote: "If it [my story] is well told and to the point, that is what I myself desired; if it is poorly done and mediocre, that was the best I could do."

# Glossary

**actualization**: The process of bringing the meaning of a biblical text into significance for the present.

**apocalypses**: Jewish writings concerned with the heavenly realm and/or the full coming of God's kingdom (e.g., the Book of Daniel, *1 Enoch*); **Apocalypse**: capitalized, it is used as a synonym for the Book of Revelation.

**Apocrypha, the**: Books of the Old Testament present in the Greek Bible tradition (e.g., Sirach, 1 and 2 Maccabees), but not in the Hebrew Bible, which have been adopted by the Catholic and Orthodox Christian canon; also called the **Deuterocanonical books** or the **Deuterocanonicals.**

**Apocryphal Gospels**: Early Christian writings from the second and third centuries (and later) ascribed to such authors as Peter, Thomas, Paul, and Mary Magdalene.

**canon**: A list of books officially sanctioned as Sacred Scripture and considered authoritative by a particular Jewish or Christian community.

**Day of Atonement** (also, in Hebrew, **Yom Kippur**): A Jewish festival celebrated in the fall during which the sins of the people are "wiped away."

**Dead Sea Scrolls**: Ancient manuscripts in Hebrew, Aramaic, and Greek discovered in the late 1940s and 1950s at several sites near the Dead Sea.

***Dei verbum***: The Latin title (meaning "Word of God") of the Dogmatic Constitution on Divine Revelation, issued by the Second Vatican Council in 1965.

**deicide**: The charge that the Jews "killed God" because they killed Jesus.

**Deuterocanonicals**: See **Apocrypha**.

*DV*—abbreviation for *Dei verbum*.

**Diaspora**: Jewish communities "scattered" outside the land of Israel.

**early Judaism**: Judaism between the time of Alexander the Great (323 BC) and the destruction of the Jerusalem temple (AD 70); early Judaism takes place within the historical period known as **Second Temple Judaism** (537 BC to AD 70).

**eschatology**: The study of the "last things." In early Jewish circles, it refers to the expectations about the future, including resurrection, the last judgment, and eternal rewards and punishment.

**Essenes**: Members of a Jewish religious movement active around Jesus' time, and generally regarded as the group behind the Qumran scrolls.

**Evangelists**: The traditional authors of the four canonical Gospels (*euangelion*)—Matthew, Mark, Luke, and John.

**Gentiles**: Non-Jewish peoples, that is, those outside of Judaism (and eventually those outside of Christianity).

**Gentile Christians**: Persons of non-Jewish heritage who became Christians.

**gospel**: First used to mean the "good news" (*euangelion*) about Jesus' death and resurrection; **Gospel**: capitalized, it refers to the four canonical narratives about Jesus.

**hermeneutics**: The science of interpretation; with regard to the Bible, it can include the whole process of interpretation, or merely the process of discerning the significance of a biblical text today.

**hierarchical**: The different sociological levels or strata in a society, with particular attention to its leaders (priests, kings, etc.).

**historical criticism**: Study of what a text meant in its original historical circumstances.

**historical Jesus, the**: The figure of the earthly Jesus as he is reconstructed by the methods of modern historical research.

**Jewish Christians**: Persons of Jewish heritage who become Christians and seek to retain many aspects of that heritage.

**justification**: A right relationship with God, made possible through Jesus' death and resurrection.

**kingdom of God**: The time when God's power will be fully manifest, and all creation will acknowledge God's absolute sovereignty.

*lectio divina*: The process of reading, meditating, praying, and contemplating and/or acting upon a biblical passage.

**Maccabees**: Jewish dynasty beginning with the brothers, Judas, Jonathan, and Simon, who were active in the late–second century BC; also the name of four of the books in the **Apocrypha**.

**Masoretic Text**: The traditional text of the Hebrew Bible; one of several textual traditions among the Qumran scrolls.

**messiah**: Means "the anointed one"; in early Jewish circles, it refers to a future leader after the pattern of David.

**Mosaic Law**: The legal requirements contained in the first five books of the Hebrew Bible; see **Torah**.

*Nostra aetate*: The Latin title (meaning "In Our Time") of the Vatican II 1965 document Declaration on the Relation of the Catholic Church to Non-Christian Religions.

**parable**: A short story about nature or everyday life, with unusual aspects leading to further reflection and a search for a deeper meaning.

**Passover**: Jewish festival celebrated in early spring to commemorate ancient Israel's liberation from slavery in Egypt.

**patriarchal**: A household ruled by a dominant male, or a society with exclusively male leadership.

**pesharim**: Biblical expositions of difficult passages in the Books of the Prophets and the Book of Psalms, found among the Qumran scrolls.

**Pharisees**: Members of a Jewish religious movement active in Israel from the second century BC to AD 70; the Gospels portray them as among Jesus' chief opponents.

**Pontifical Biblical Commission**: An international group of Catholic biblical scholars that advises the pope on biblical matters, and issues statements on important topics pertaining to the Bible.

**Pontius Pilate**: The Roman prefect, or governor, of Palestine between AD 26 and 36.

**prophet**: One who speaks on God's behalf about the present and/or the future.

**Pseudepigrapha**: Second Temple Jewish writings (falsely) ascribed to ancient figures such as Enoch, Moses, and Solomon.

**Q**: The symbol given to the hypothetical collection of sayings attributed to Jesus and used independently by Matthew and by Luke.

**Qumran**: The site near the Dead Sea where the most important scrolls were found in the late 1940s and 1950s.

**rabbinic writings**: Collections of Jewish traditions preserved in the Mishnah, the Talmuds, and the Midrashim.

**rabbis**: Jewish teachers active from the time of Jesus to the seventh century AD.

**redaction criticism**: Study of how an author incorporated sources, and what point(s) he wanted to make in doing so.

**resurrection**: Restoration to life from death of the whole person (body and soul) for eternal life.

**Roman Empire**: Territories (including Palestine) ruled directly by the Roman emperors, beginning with Augustus in the late first century BC.

**Second Temple Judaism**: Period in Jewish history from the return from exile in 537 BC to the destruction of Jerusalem and its temple in AD 70; see **early Judaism**.

**Septuagint**: Greek versions of the Hebrew Bible made in Alexandria in Egypt from the third century BC onward.

**Sermon on the Mount**: Jesus' wisdom instruction in Matthew 5–7.

**Shoah**: The catastrophic destruction visited upon European Jews under the Nazis in the mid-twentieth century.

**synod**: An occasional gathering of Catholic bishops to advise the pope on matters of current ecclesial concern.

**Synoptic Gospels**: Term applied to the Gospels of Matthew, Mark, and Luke because of their "common vision" of Jesus.

**Teacher of Righteousness**: A major figure in some Qumran scrolls who is thought to have provided spiritual leadership for the community there.

**Third Quest**: The most recent phase in the quest for the historical Jesus that began in the mid-1980s and emphasized the Jewishness of Jesus.

**Torah**: From the Hebrew for "instruction," the word may refer to the first five books in the Hebrew Bible, or merely to the legal requirements in them; see **Mosaic Law**.

**Two-Source Theory**: The proposed solution to the problematic relationships among the Synoptics (that is, the first three Gospels), according to which Matthew and Luke, working independently, both used the Gospel of Mark and Q as sources, and then individually also used other sources designated as M and L, respectively.

**works of the law**: May refer to all the laws in the Torah, or (more restrictively) to what made Jews distinctive in the Greco-Roman world: circumcision, Sabbath observance, and ritual purity laws.

**Yom Kippur.** See **Day of Atonement.**

# General Bibliography

Barton, John. *The Nature of Biblical Criticism*. Louisville, KY: Westminster John Knox, 2007. An even-handed introduction to the historical method of biblical interpretation.

Béchard, Dean, ed. *The Scripture Documents: An Anthology of Official Catholic Teachings*. Collegeville, MN: Liturgical Press, 2002. An excellent anthology of official Catholic documents on biblical interpretation.

Benedict XVI, Pope. *Verbum Domini: The Word of God in the Life and Mission of the Church*. Ijamsville, MD: Word Among Us Press, 2010. A powerful synthesis of recent Catholic documents on the place of the Bible in the church and in the world.

Bilde, Per. *Flavius Josephus between Jerusalem and Rome: His Life, His Works, and Their Importance*. Sheffield, UK: JSOT Press, 1998. A lively introduction to reading the works of Josephus.

Brettler, Marc, Peter Enns, and Daniel J. Harrington. *The Bible and the Believer: How to Read the Bible Critically and Religiously*. New York: Oxford University Press, 2012. How three scholars—Jewish, Catholic, and Evangelical—combine the critical and religious approaches to the Bible.

Brown, Raymond E. *An Introduction to New Testament Christology*. New York: Paulist Press, 1994. An excellent description of how the tradition about Jesus developed in its early phases.

———. *The Death of the Messiah*. 2 vols. New York: Doubleday, 1994, 1999. The most comprehensive analysis of the New Testament passion narratives.

———. *The Community of the Beloved Disciple*. New York: Paulist Press, 1979. A groundbreaking work on the history of the community that produced John's Gospel and Letters.

Bryan, Christopher. *Render to Caesar: Jesus, the Early Church, and the Roman Superpower*. New York: Oxford University Press, 2005. A balanced perspective on the biblical passages that pertain to the relation between church and state.

Byrne, Brendan. *Romans*. Collegeville, MN: Liturgical Press, 1996. An excellent historical, literary, and theological commentary on Paul's most important letter.

Carson, Donald A., Peter T. O'Brien, and Mark A. Seifrid, eds. *Justification and Variegated Nomism*. 2 vols. Grand Rapids: Baker, 2001, 2004. Essays by distinguished Evangelical scholars who are critical of the New Perspective on Paul.

Charlesworth, James H., ed. *The Old Testament Pseudepigrapha*. 2 vols. New York: Doubleday, 1983, 1985. Introductions, translations, and notes on important early Jewish texts.

Collins, John J., and Daniel C. Harlow, eds. *The Eerdmans Dictionary of Early Judaism*. Grand Rapids: Eerdmans, 2010. The best available guide to scholarship on the Jewish world of the New Testament.

Collins, Raymond F. *First Corinthians*. Collegeville, MN: Liturgical Press, 1999. Places Paul's letter in its Jewish and Greco-Roman contexts.

Donahue, John R., and Daniel J. Harrington. *The Gospel of Mark*. Collegeville, MN: Liturgical Press, 2002. A historical, literary, and theological commentary on the earliest Gospel.

Dunn, James G. D. *The New Perspective on Paul*. Rev. ed. Tübingen: Mohr Siebeck, 2005. Essays on various topics by one of the pioneers in the New Perspective on Paul.

—————. *Jesus Remembered*. Grand Rapids: Eerdmans, 2003. Contends that what we have in the New Testament are remembrances about Jesus, that is, how he was remembered.

Elliott, J. Keith, ed. *The Apocryphal Jesus: Legends of the Early Church*. Oxford: Oxford University Press, 1996. Introductions, translations, and notes for ancient noncanonical works about Jesus.

Elliott, John H. *A Home for the Homeless: A Social-Scientific Criticism of 1 Peter, Its Situation and Strategy*. Minneapolis: Fortress, 1990. Argues that 1 Peter addressed migrants seeking and finding a home in the church.

Fiore, Benjamin. *The Pastoral Epistles: First Timothy, Second Timothy, Titus.* Collegeville, MN: Liturgical Press, 2007. Places the Pastorals especially in the context of Greco-Roman moral philosophy.

Fiorenza, Elisabeth Schüssler. *In Memory of Her: A Feminist Theological Reconstruction of Christian Origins.* New York: Continuum, 1994. A pioneering work in highlighting the role of women in the Jesus movement.

Gadamer, Hans-Georg. *Truth and Method.* New York: Seabury, 1975. The classic work on hermeneutics in general by a famous philosopher.

Harrington, Daniel J. *Jesus: A Historical Portrait.* Cincinnati, OH: St. Anthony Messenger Press, 2007. A synthesis of modern scholarship on Jesus for a nonspecialist audience.

————. *How Do Catholics Read the Bible?* Lanham, MD: Rowman & Littlefield, 2005. Shows how *Dei Verbum* has affected and enriched Catholic biblical interpretation.

————. *Invitation to the Apocrypha.* Grand Rapids: Eerdmans, 1999. Provides introductions to and interpretations of the Old Testament books contained in the Catholic and Orthodox canons of Scripture but not in the Hebrew Bible.

————. *The Gospel of Matthew.* Collegeville, MN: Liturgical Press, 1991. A commentary that emphasizes Matthew's setting in Judaism, and its significance for Christian-Jewish relations today.

————. *Interpreting the New Testament: A Practical Guide.* Collegeville, MN: Liturgical Press, 1990. A guide to understanding and applying the different exegetical methods to specific texts.

Harrington, Wilfrid J. *Revelation.* Collegeville, MN: Liturgical Press, 1993. A concise reading of Apocalypse, the Book of Revelation, with a special interest in its theology.

Hartin, Patrick. *James.* Collegeville, MN: Liturgical Press, 2003. A close reading of the letter from James with reference to both its Jewish roots and its place in early Christianity and the Greco-Roman world.

Hays, Richard B. *The Faith of Jesus Christ: The Narrative Substratum of Galatians 3:1—4:11*. Rev. ed. Grand Rapids: Eerdmans, 2002. The first full-scale treatment of reading "the faith of Christ" as a subjective genitive.

Hengel, Martin. *Between Jesus and Paul: Studies in the Earliest History of Christianity*. Philadelphia: Fortress, 1983. Essays tracing the development of the church from the earliest post-Easter community in Jerusalem to Paul's mission.

—————. *Judaism and Hellenism: Studies in Their Encounter in Palestine during the Early Hellenistic Period*. 2 vols. Philadelphia: Fortress, 1974. The classic treatment of early Greek influence in Palestine in the period before Jesus.

Hengel, Martin, and Anna Maria Schwemer. *Paul between Damascus and Antioch: The Unknown Years*. Louisville, KY: Westminster John Knox, 1997. Covers Paul's career between his conversion and his early activity in Antioch up to the Apostolic Council, that is, between AD 33 and 49.

Hoppe, Leslie. *There Shall Be No Poor Among You: Poverty in the Bible*. Nashville: Abingdon, 2004. Fine treatment of the themes of poverty and riches in the Bible.

Horsley, Richard A. *Jesus and the Spiral of Violence: Popular Jewish Resistance in Roman Palestine*. Minneapolis: Fortress, 1992. Stimulating reconstruction of political ferment in Palestine in Jesus' time and before.

Johnson, Luke Timothy. *The Acts of the Apostles*. Collegeville, MN: Liturgical Press, 1992. An excellent literary and theological analysis of the Acts of the Apostles; is also the companion volume to, and continuation of, the item below.

—————. *The Gospel of Luke*. Collegeville, MN: Liturgical Press, 1991. An excellent literary and theological analysis of Luke's Gospel.

Kamesar, Adam, ed. *The Cambridge Companion to Philo*. New York / Cambridge, UK: Cambridge University Press, 2010. Essays on various aspects of Philo's works by distinguished scholars.

Kim, Seyoon. *Paul and the New Perspective*. Grand Rapids: Eerdmans, 2002. An Evangelical critique of many elements in the New Perspective on Paul.

Lim, Timothy H. *Holy Scripture in the Qumran Commentaries and Pauline Letters.* Oxford: Clarendon Press, 1997. Analysis of how Scripture was used in certain texts of the Dead Sea Scrolls and in Paul's letters.

MacDonald, Margaret Y. *Colossians and Ephesians.* Collegeville, MN: Liturgical Press, 2000. A fine commentary, distinctive for its social-scientific reading of the texts.

Magness, Jodi. *Stone and Dung, Oil and Spit: Jewish Daily Life in the Time of Jesus.* Grand Rapids: Eerdmans, 2011. An excellent treatment based on archaeological and literary sources.

Matera, Frank J. *New Testament Theology: Exploring Unity and Diversity.* Louisville, KY: Westminster John Knox, 2007. Does justice to the individual theological perspectives in the New Testament, and the themes that unify them.

————. *Galatians.* Collegeville, MN: Liturgical Press, 1992. A concise commentary, integrating many of the new perspectives on Paul.

Meeks, Wayne A. *The First Urban Christians: The Social World of the Apostle Paul.* New Haven, CT: Yale University Press, 2003. The best introduction to what it felt like to be an early Christian in the Greco-Roman world.

Meier, John P. *A Marginal Jew: Rethinking the Historical Jesus.* Vols. 1–4. New York: Doubleday / New Haven, CT: Yale University Press, 1991–2009. A very detailed analysis of the teachings and actions of Jesus according to the Synoptic Gospels, with a strong concern for their Jewish setting.

Mitchell, Alan C. *Hebrews.* Collegeville, MN: Liturgical Press, 2007. A fine exposition of the Letter to the Hebrews, with particular attention to its literary and theological dimensions.

Moloney, Francis J. *The Gospel of John.* Collegeville, MN: Liturgical Press, 1998. A narrative commentary on John's Gospel by a great Johannine expert.

Pelikan, Jaroslav. *Interpreting the Bible & the Constitution.* New Haven, CT: Yale University Press, 2004. A fascinating comparison between biblical and legal interpretation by a famous historian of Christian theology.

Pilgrim, Walter E. *Uneasy Neighbors: Church and State in the New Testament.* Minneapolis: Fortress, 1999. A balanced and careful reading of the "church and state" texts.

Räisänen, Heikki. *Paul and the Law.* Tübingen: Mohr Siebeck, 1983. Makes the claim that in his teachings about the Jewish Law, Paul was ambiguous and probably confused.

Ratzinger, Joseph (Pope Benedict XVI). *Jesus of Nazareth.* 2 vols. New York: Doubleday, 2008; San Francisco: Ignatius Press, 2011. Masterful reflections on various episodes in the Gospels, combining biblical exegesis and the theological tradition.

Ryan, Judith M., and Bonnie B. Thurston. *Philippians & Philemon.* Collegeville, MN: Liturgical Press, 2005. Excellent expositions of two somewhat neglected Pauline letters, Ryan on Philemon, and Thurston on Philippians.

Saldarini, Anthony J. *Pharisees, Scribes, and Sadducees: A Sociological Approach.* Rev. ed. Grand Rapids: Eerdmans, 2001. Fine description of the Jewish groups contemporary with Jesus.

————. *Matthew's Christian-Jewish Community.* Chicago: University of Chicago Press, 1994. Brilliant reading of Matthew's Gospel in the context of early Judaism and the early stages of the rabbinic movement.

Sanders, E. P. *Jesus and Judaism.* Philadelphia: Fortress, 1985. A pioneering work that can be said to have initiated the Third Quest.

————. *Paul and Palestinian Judaism: A Comparison of Patterns of Religion.* Philadelphia: Fortress, 1977. Another pioneering work that can be said to have initiated the New Perspective on Paul.

Schneiders, Sandra M. *The Revelatory Text: Interpreting the New Testament as Sacred Scripture.* Rev. ed. Collegeville, MN: Liturgical Press, 1999. An excellent presentation about how hermeneutical theory can be used profitably in New Testament interpretation.

Schreiner, Thomas R. *New Testament Theology: Magnifying God in Christ.* Grand Rapids: Baker Academic, 2008. A comprehensive thematic theology of the New Testament from a distinguished Evangelical scholar.

Schweitzer, Albert. *The Quest of the Historical Jesus.* Minneapolis: Fortress, 2001. The classic description of the First Quest from one of the great figures of the twentieth century.

Segal, Alan. *Paul the Convert: The Apostolate and Apostasy of Saul the Pharisee.* New Haven, CT: Yale University Press, 1990. A distinguished Jewish scholar tries to locate Paul in the context of the Judaism of his time.

Senior, Donald, and Daniel J. Harrington. *1 Peter, Jude and 2 Peter.* Collegeville, MN: Liturgical Press, 2003. Commentaries on three somewhat neglected letters from literary, historical, and theological perspectives.

Stendahl, Krister. *Paul among Jews and Gentiles.* Philadelphia: Fortress, 1976. Imaginative essays by a Swedish Lutheran scholar and bishop that were foundational for developing the New Perspective on Paul.

Strack, Hermann L., and Günter Stemberger. *Introduction to the Talmud and Midrash.* Edinburgh: T&T Clark, 1991. The standard guidebook to the rabbinic writings.

Theissen, Gerd. *The Religion of the Earliest Churches.* Minneapolis: Fortress, 1999. Looks at early Christianity from the perspectives of its doctrines, rituals, and ethical teachings.

VanderKam, James C. *The Dead Sea Scrolls Today.* Grand Rapids: Eerdmans, 2010. A reliable and up-to-date handbook on the Qumran scrolls.

Vermes, Geza. *The Complete Dead Sea Scrolls in English.* London: Penguin Books, 2004. Now the standard work, it contains an extensive introduction to the Qumran texts and reliable English translations.

Williamson, Peter S. *Catholic Principles for Interpreting Scripture: A Study of the Pontifical Biblical Commission's "The Interpretation of the Bible in the Church."* Rome: Biblical Institute Press, 2001. An extensive commentary on a very important Catholic document on methodology in biblical interpretation.

Witherington, Ben. *Jesus the Sage: The Pilgrimage of Wisdom.* Minneapolis: Fortress, 1994. Places Jesus the wisdom teacher in the context of the biblical tradition of wisdom.

Wright, N. T. *Justification: God's Plan and Paul's Vision.* Downers Grove, IL: InterVarsity Academic, 2009. Wright responds to Evangelical critics of his version of the New Perspective on Paul.

————. *The Resurrection of the Son of God.* Minneapolis: Fortress, 2003. A comprehensive analysis of the texts and traditions about resurrection, and a defense of the Gospel narratives.

————. *Jesus and the Victory of God.* Minneapolis: Fortress, 1997. An Anglican scholar and bishop interprets Jesus and his self-consciousness in terms of the great traditions of Israel.

# Index of Authors

Barton, John, 8, 107
Béchard, Dean, 3, 5, 107
Benedict XVI (Pope), 4–5, 11, 45–46, 107, 112
Bilde, Per, 24, 107
Brettler, Marc, 2, 107
Brown, Raymond E., 41, 48, 60, 107
Bryan, Christopher, 39, 108
Byrne, Brendan, 86, 108

Carson, Donald A., 79, 108
Charlesworth, James H., 22, 24, 108
Collins, John J., 16, 108
Collins, Raymond F., 92, 108

Donahue, John R., 56, 108
Dunn, James G. D., 53, 77, 108

Elliott, James Keith, 61, 108
Elliott, John H., 90, 108
Enns, Peter, 2, 107

Fiore, Benjamin, 93, 109
Fiorenza, Elisabeth Schüssler, 40, 109

Gadamer, Hans-Georg, 7, 109

Harlow, Daniel C., 16, 108
Harrington, Daniel J., 2, 3, 8, 21, 27, 33, 56, 57, 88, 107, 108, 109, 113
Harrington, Wilfrid J., 109
Hartin, Patrick, 87, 109
Hays, Richard B., 74, 110
Hengel, Martin, 26, 48, 71, 110
Hoppe, Leslie, 39, 110
Horsley, Richard A., 39

Johnson, Luke Timothy, 58, 83, 110

Kamesar, Adam, 24, 110
Kim, Seyoon, 79, 110

Lim, Timothy H., 66, 111

MacDonald, Margaret Y., 94, 111
Magness, Jodi, 25, 111
Matera, Frank J., 12, 86, 111
Meeks, Wayne A., 81, 111
Meier, John P., 32, 38, 111
Mitchell, Alan C., 88, 111
Moloney, Francis J., 60, 111

O'Brien, Peter T., 108

Pelikan, Jaroslav, 6, 111
Pilgrim, Walter E., , 82, 112

Räisänen, Heikki, 68, 112
Ratzinger, Joseph, 4, 45, 112; see also Benedict XVI
Ryan, Judith M., , 95, 112

Saldarini, Anthony J., , 70, 88, 112
Sanders, E. P., 32, 67, 112
Schneiders, Sandra M., , 7, 112
Schreiner, Thomas R., , 13, 112
Schweitzer, Albert, 31, 46, 113
Schwemer, Anna Maria, 71, 110
Segal, Alan, 70, 113

Seifrid, Mark A., , 108
Senior, Donald, 89, 113
Stemberger, Günter, 25, 113
Stendahl, Krister, 69, 113
Strack, Hermann L., , 25, 113

Theissen, Gerd, 48, 113
Thurston, Bonnie B., , 112

VanderKam, James C., , 17, 113
Vermes, Geza, 17, 113

Williamson, Peter S., , 5, 113
Witherington, Ben, 35, 114
Wright, N. T., , 32, 43, 73, 114

# Index of Scripture, Church Documents, and Ancient Texts

**SCRIPTURE**

**Genesis**

| | |
|---|---|
| 1–11 | 66 |
| 5:24 | 23 |
| 14 | 89 |
| 17 | 66 |
| 17:5 | 66 |

**Deuteronomy**

| | |
|---|---|
| 24:1–4 | 41 |

**Exodus**

| | |
|---|---|
| 19:6 | 90 |

**Psalms**

| | |
|---|---|
| 8 | 89 |
| 97:1 | 35 |
| 110 | 89 |

**Proverbs**

| | |
|---|---|
| 1–9 | 87 |
| 8 | 49 |
| 22–24 | 87 |

**Wisdom**

| | |
|---|---|
| 3:1 | 22 |

**Sirach**

| | |
|---|---|
| 24 | 49 |

**Isaiah**

| | |
|---|---|
| 6:9–10 | 78 |
| 53 | 49, 91 |

**Jeremiah**

| | |
|---|---|
| 1:5 | 71 |

**Daniel**

| | |
|---|---|
| 12:2 | 44 |

**2 Maccabees**

| | |
|---|---|
| 7 | 44 |
| 15:38 | 100 |

**Matthew**

| | |
|---|---|
| 3:7–10 | 51 |
| 5–7 | 36, 50, 57, 104 |
| 5:33–37 | 87 |
| 6:10 | 35 |
| 6:19 | 37 |
| 10 | 57 |
| 13 | 57 |
| 14:31 | 58 |

| | |
|---|---|
| 16:17–19 | 58 |
| 18 | 57 |
| 19:10–12 | 41 |
| 22:15–22 | 39 |
| 24 | 36, 58 |
| 24–25 | 57, 58 |
| 25 | 36, 58 |
| 28:19 | 88 |

**Mark**

| | |
|---|---|
| 1:1—8:21 | 56 |
| 1:15 | 34, 57 |
| 2:1—3:6 | 50 |
| 3:22–30 | 38 |
| 4 | 36 |
| 4:30–32 | 36 |
| 6:3 | 34 |
| 8:22—10:52 | 56 |
| 8:29 | 56 |
| 10:2–12 | 41 |
| 11:1–11, 15–19 | 37 |
| 11:1—16:8 | 56 |
| 12:13–17 | 37, 39, 82 |
| 12:18–27 | 44 |
| 13 | 58 |
| 13:1–2 | 43 |
| 13:1–31 | 57 |
| 13:32–37 | 57 |
| 14:32–42 | 74 |
| 14:61–62 | 43 |
| 15:40–41 | 57 |

**Luke**

| | |
|---|---|
| 1–2 | 40 |
| 1:1–4 | xvi |
| 2:1 | 81 |
| 3:1 | 81 |
| 3:7–9 | 51 |

| | |
|---|---|
| 4:16–30 | 59 |
| 7:16 | 59 |
| 8:2–3 | 40, 59 |
| 9:51—19:27 | 59 |
| 9:53 | 59 |
| 10:25–37 | 33 |
| 10:30–37 | 36 |
| 10:38–42 | 40 |
| 11:20 | 35, 38 |
| 11:28 | 40 |
| 13:10–17 | 41 |
| 13:33 | 59 |
| 15:11–32 | 36 |
| 17:21 | 35 |
| 20:20–26 | 39 |
| 21:5–6 | 59 |
| 23:34 | 59 |
| 23:42 | 59 |
| 23:46 | 59 |
| 24:25–27 | 59 |

**John**

| | |
|---|---|
| 1 | 34 |
| 1:1 | xvi |
| 1:1–18 | 60 |
| 1:14 | 16, 33 |
| 2–12 | 50, 60 |
| 2:1–11 | 61 |
| 4:1–42 | 33 |
| 13–17 | 50 |
| 13–21 | 60 |
| 19:25–27 | 61 |

**Acts of the Apostles**

| | |
|---|---|
| 1–8 | 84 |
| 1:8 | 83 |
| 9 | 70, 84 |
| 10–11 | 71 |

| | | | |
|---|---|---|---|
| 10:1—11:18 | 84 | 7 | 92 |
| 13:1—14:28 | 84 | 8–10 | 92 |
| 15 | xiv, 72, 84 | 11 | 93 |
| 15:29 | 72 | 12–14 | 93 |
| 15:41—18:22 | 84 | 12:7 | 93 |
| 18:23—20:38 | 84 | 13:12 | 29 |
| 20:35 | 61 | 15:3–5 | 49 |
| 22 | 70, 84 | 15:3–8 | 44 |
| 26 | 70, 84 | | |
| 28:31 | 84 | **Galatians** | |
| | | 1 | 70 |
| **Romans** | | 1:13–17 | 68 |
| 1 | 66, 75 | 1:14 | 65, 68 |
| 1:16 | 75 | 1:15 | 71 |
| 2:1—3:8 | 75 | 1:16 | 71 |
| 3:9 | 75 | 3:1–5 | 72, 86 |
| 3:10–18 | 75 | 3:2 | 76 |
| 3:22 | 74 | 3:6–29 | 77 |
| 3:25 | 49 | 3:16 | 72 |
| 3:31 | 67 | 3:19–20 | 68 |
| 7 | 69 | 3:24–25 | 67 |
| 7:7–25 | 68 | 3:28 | 49 |
| 7:12 | 67 | 4:10 | 77 |
| 9–11 | 77, 78, 86, 99 | 5:1 | 86 |
| 9:1–5 | 77 | 5:6 | 77, 87 |
| 11:1–16 | 78 | 5:12 | 77 |
| 11:17–24 | 78 | 6:13 | 77 |
| 11:25–26 | 77, 78, 87 | | |
| 11:26 | 78 | **Ephesians** | |
| 13:1–7 | 82 | 5:21—6:9 | 94 |
| 13:11–14 | 82 | | |
| 15:24 | 84 | **Philippians** | |
| | | 2:6–11 | 49 |
| **1 Corinthians** | | 3 | 69, 70 |
| 1–4 | 92 | 3:2–16 | 68 |
| 1:18–25 | 92 | 3:5–6 | 65 |
| 3:5–17 | 92 | 3:6 | 69 |
| 5–6 | 92 | 3:7–8 | 66 |

| | | | |
|---|---|---|---|
| 3:8 | 69 | 1:22 | 87 |
| 3:10–11 | 69 | 1:27 | 87 |
| | | 2:1 | 87 |
| **Colossians** | | 2:1–7 | 88 |
| 1:15–20 | 49 | 2:10–13 | 87 |
| 3:18—4:1 | 94 | 2:14–26 | 87 |
| | | 5:1–6 | 88 |
| **1 Timothy** | | 5:12 | 87 |
| 2:2 | 82, 93 | | |
| 2:5–6 | 94 | **1 Peter** | |
| 2:8–15 | 94 | 1:2 | 90 |
| 2:12 | 94 | 1:3–9 | 90 |
| 3:15 | 94 | 1:14 | 90 |
| 3:16 | 94 | 1:17–18 | 90 |
| 5:3–16 | 94 | 1:18 | 90 |
| | | 2:9 | 90 |
| **Philemon** | | 2:10 | 90 |
| v. 16 | 96 | 2:11–12 | 91 |
| v. 21 | 96 | 2:13–14, 17 | 83 |
| | | 2:21–25 | 91 |
| **Hebrews** | | 4:3–4 | 91 |
| 1:1—4:13 | 89 | 4:13–19 | 91 |
| 4:14—10:18 | 89 | 5:12 | 91 |
| 10:19—13:25 | 89 | | |
| 10:32–34 | 89 | **Revelation** | |
| 12:2 | 89 | 4–5 | 28 |
| 12:4 | 89 | 12–13 | 83 |
| | | 17–18 | 83 |
| **James** | | 17:1 | 83 |
| 1:1 | 87 | | |

**CHURCH DOCUMENTS**

*Dei verbum*, xiii, xvi, 1, 2–5, 14, 45, 47, 98, 100, 101, 109
*Divino Afflante Spiritu*, 3
*Interpretation of the Bible in the Church, The*, 5, 113
*Nostra aetate*, 4, 65, 99, 103
*Verbum Domini*, 5, 107

**ANCIENT TEXTS**
**The Apocrypha (or Deuterocanonical Books)**
Additions to the Book of Daniel, 22
Additions to the Book of Esther, 22
Baruch, 22
Ecclesiasticus. *See* Sirach
Judith, 21
1 Maccabees, 22, 101
2 Maccabees, 22, 44, 100, 101
Sirach, 21, 22, 36, 49
Tobit, 17, 21
Wisdom, Book of, 22, 44, 49

**Old Testament Pseudepigrapha**
*Apocalypse of Abraham*, 24
*2 Baruch*, 24, 35, 66
*Biblical Antiquities*, 24
*1 Enoch*, 17, 23, 27, 35, 101, 104; "Book of the Giants," 23; "Book of Parables," 23; "Similitudes of Enoch," 23
*2 Enoch*, 24

*3 Enoch*, 24
*4 Ezra*, 24, 35, 66
*Joseph and Aseneth*, 24
*Jubilees*, 17, 24
*Life of Adam and Eve*, 24
*4 Maccabees*, 24
*Prayer of Manasseh*, 24
*Psalms of Solomon*, 24
*Sentences of ps.-Phocylides*, 24
*Testament of Levi*, 17–18
*Testament of Moses*, 24
*Testament of Solomon*, 24
*Testaments of the Twelve Patriarchs*, 24

**Apocryphal Gospels**
*Gospel of Judas*, 62
*Gospel of Mary*, 62
*Gospel of Peter*, 22, 62
*Gospel of Philip*, 62
*Gospel of Thomas*, 62, 63
*Infancy Gospel of Thomas*, 62
*Protoevangelium of James*, 62

**The Dead Sea Scrolls**
*Copper Scroll*, 18
*Damascus Document*, 18,
*Genesis Apocryphon*, 17
*Hodayot*, 28
*4QInstruction*, 18
*Rule of the Community*, 18, 28, 75
*Temple Scroll*, 18
*Thanksgiving Hymns*, 18, 28
*War Scroll*, 18, 27

**Other Ancient Texts**
Babylonian Talmud, 24
*Jewish Antiquities*, 24
*Jewish War, The*, 24
*Life of Josephus Flavius*, 24

Midrashim, 24
Mishnah, 24
Palestinian Talmud, 24
Targumim, 17, 25